STATE OF CONNECTICUT

D & NEW YORK RAIL ROAD

rtifies that *Drake Mead*

Shares of **FIFTY**

the *Capital Stock* of the **RIDGEFIELD & NEW**

MBER

12

011

SHA

HARTFORD AND NEW HAVEN
RAILROAD COMPANY

it Known, That *John M. Belden of New*

entitled to One — Shar

TAL STOCK of the **HARTFORD AND**

EN RAILROAD COMPANY,

No. 2541

14 **For Value**

Gilman So

all my right, tit

(a

of the **NAUGATU**

been paid **ONE HUN**

Bridgeport Ju

DANBURY & NORWALK

AND COM

ties this

d to Fifteen — Shares of Fif

Capital Stock of the Danbury and Norwalk

and Massachusetts
MASSACHUSETTS DIVISION,

tify that *S. A. Hudson*

One — Sha

THE
COLLECTOR'S BOOK
OF THE
LOCOMOTIVE

Other Books by EDWIN P. ALEXANDER

MODEL RAILROADS
IRON HORSES: *American Locomotives 1829–1905*
AMERICAN LOCOMOTIVES: *A Pictorial Record of Steam Power 1900–1950*
THE PENNSYLVANIA RAILROAD: *A Pictorial History*

THE
COLLECTOR'S BOOK

OF THE
LOCOMOTIVE

EDWIN P. ALEXANDER

 Bramhall House · New York

Unless otherwise accredited,
all photographs are those of the author.

This edition published by Bramhall House,
a division of Clarkson N. Potter, Inc.
C D E F G H

This is for Maggy

Contents

THE
COLLECTOR'S BOOK
OF THE
LOCOMOTIVE

Preface

THE IRON HORSE WAS NO MORE THAN A GANGLING colt when, universally capturing imaginations, it began to be woven as a theme into many objects familiar to man. From the very early contemporary paintings and prints, which appeared shortly after the birth of the engine, to modern times, its likeness may be found in both decorative and useful objects. It was also often depicted as a fascinating symbol of speed, power, and the ingenuity of man.

Because the subject was so diversely reproduced, it is only natural that collectors of railroadiana would develop classifications into which representations of the steam locomotive fall. The largest groupings are generally those comprising prints, photographs, toys, and scale models. But while these categories are accordingly given most space in this book, the lesser-known groups are not neglected, for my purpose is to show how variously and widely the locomotive's likeness has been duplicated.

Not only devotees of the iron horse, but I think, most people enjoy seeing the locomotive in any form, especially now, as its kind becomes obsolete. Undoubtedly some of the reproductions shown here will be new to readers other than genuine enthusiasts, but even the latter will find some unknown or different variations of their favorite subject. And with the exception of some toys, only the steam locomotive is depicted.

Addict that I am, compiling the contents of this book has been a truly enjoyable experience for me. There is a minimum of text, for I subscribe to the supposedly Chinese saying, "One picture is worth ten thousand words." Now that the days of the steam locomotive are numbered, perhaps this tribute to its worldwide influence will help in some measure to perpetuate its memory and aid its admirers in their respective hobbies.

chapter I

The Locomotive in Art

BEFORE THE ADVENT OF PHOTOGRAPHY, the iron horse was, fortunately, depicted in various mediums, and we are well acquainted with its earliest forms. There were crude woodcuts, sometimes inaccurate; occasionally an artist who had never even seen the new machine drew what purported to be one. There were good woodcuts, too, and there were copperplate etchings; but steel engravings were probably the best, and usually the most accurate, representations of contemporary locomotives. Many are to be found in old engineering textbooks, and some of the larger ones in folio sizes should be classed with lithographs or prints for their interest and value.

Sometimes the delineator of an engraving or print is of more than casual interest, thus increasing the significance of his work. Such was Charles Blacker Vignoles, who pictured the "Novelty" (page 10) in 1829 and who is credited in Europe as the inventor of the flat-bottom rail, which he conceived independently of Robert Stevens, America's pioneer designer of this rail. The "Novelty," one of the unsuccessful entries in the Rainhill Trials of 1829, did run quite well, up to fifty miles an hour, but mechanical failure eliminated it. John Ericsson, then only twenty-six, its designer and builder with John Braithwaite, was later to become more famous as the inventor of the screw propeller and builder of the ironclad *Monitor*. Vignoles's opinion of this pioneer iron horse should be noted: "The 'Novelty' was long remembered as the beau ideal of a locomotive, which, if it did not command success, deserved it."

Another engineer and draftsman in the early days of locomotive development was L. Hinkley of Boston, a member of the family of engine builders of that name. Their lithographs were the work of B. W. Thayer & Company.

The prints most interesting and desired among collectors, whether lovers of engines or fanciers of Americana, are the contemporary lithographs issued by locomotive builders such as Baldwin, Rogers, the various New England and some Midwestern firms. These colorful prints, far more accurate than the familiar Currier & Ives railroad scenes, are our best clues to the elegant planning, workmanship, and coloring practiced by the iron-horse designers of a century ago.

Because collectors are so eager for these beautiful lithographs, and because comparatively few are available, their value has steadily increased. For that matter, so has that of Currier & Ives prints, but general scarcity rather than fidelity to the subject basically determines print prices among dealers. Some of the Currier & Ives artists were more exacting than others in depicting the iron horse, but there is no general rule applicable as to which are the more historically correct; only a student of the locomotive's development can decide that.

Some of the lithographers, other than Currier & Ives, of locomotive prints through the 1850s and 1860s were:

AMERICAN BANK NOTE COMPANY	New York
J. BIEN	New York
T. BOWEN	Philadelphia
A. BRETT	Philadelphia
J. H. BUFFORD	Boston
CLAY, COSSACK & COMPANY	Buffalo
P. S. DUVAL	New York
ENDICOTT & COMPANY OR ENDICOTT & SMETT	New York
GRAPHIC COMPANY	New York
F. HEPPENHEIMER	New York
HOEN & COMPANY	Richmond
MIDDLETON, WALLACE & COMPANY OR MIDDLETON, STROWBRIDGE & COMPANY	Cincinnati
JAS. R. OSGOOD & COMPANY	Boston
L. N. ROSENTHAL	Philadelphia
SAGE SONS & COMPANY	Buffalo
T. SINCLAIR	New York
B. W. THAYER & COMPANY	Boston
THOMAS & COMPANY	New York
ED WEBER	Baltimore

Generally, all American lithographs, colored or not, are of interest to all collectors of Americana. Certain English and continental prints, too, are just as interesting and scarce, becoming almost as much sought after. The popularity of all types of railroad prints is also evidenced by their frequent reissues, many for calendar use and for other advertising.

In paintings there are, unfortunately, all too few really excellent likenesses of early iron horses. Among the outstanding works are those of Edward Lamson Henry, some of which are to be seen at the Metropolitan Museum of Art in

New York. Other well-known artists whose paintings of trains are familiar are Sheldon Pennoyer, some of these having appeared in *Fortune,* and Grif Teller, Walter L. Greens, and Leslie Ragan, whose calendar paintings for the Pennsylvania and New York Central are famous.

Once in a while an artist draws or paints a historical scene showing a locomotive that is erroneous or anachronistic. A good example is the famous "General," which is often depicted being chased by the "Texas," both engines appearing as they look today. Actually, the "General" looks very little as it did in the 1860s at the time of the Andrews Raid, for various repairs and rebuildings have given it the appearance of any 4-4-0 type of the 1870s. To be historically accurate, a scene of that chase must show everything as it then existed. When the locomotives are incorrectly depicted, the Union soldiers might as well, for instance, wear the uniforms of the Rough Riders. Actually, through a reasonable amount of research, an artist could have found a Brady photograph of the "General," taken in the same year as the chase, upon which a true representation might have been made. In 1914 two such watercolors by Wilbur G. Kurtz (reproduced in Freeman Hubbard's *Railroad Avenue*) reflected good research by the artist, and did proper justice to the subject.

On the other hand, there are contemporary artists and illustrators who do painstaking research in order to have their versions of the iron horse as perfect as possible. Among them, for instance, was Frank Godwin, whose "Rusty Riley" had occasional adventures involving trains. As a lover of locomotives, Mr. Godwin has painted, etched, and built live-steam models of them (pages 28 and 164). The period railroad scenes of another well-known artist and etcher, George Bradshaw, show similar meticulous accuracy. Other artists who have more or less specialized in railroad subjects, and excellently, are E. S. Hammack, Howard Fogg, Frederick Blakeslee, Philip Ronfor, Herb Mott, Aurion Proctur, Henry Comstock, and M. C. Merritt.

Cartoons as a form of art quite frequently use railroads and model railroads for their theme. These are not new in concept, for over the past hundred years there have been many political cartoons with this subject. Later on, the machinations of the Goulds, Vanderbilts, and others provided fertile ground for cartoons, and numerous drawings decried the frequency of train wrecks in the early days before safety became the watchword. In more modern times, the trend seems to have turned almost wholly toward the humorous types (pages 27 and 127).

Some mechanical drawings of iron horses are so beautifully detailed, and the delineation so expertly done, that their inclusion as art is permissible. Those of Grafton Greenough, who, spurred by his inherent love for the locomotive from childhood, rose through the ranks at Baldwin's to become vice president, are perfect examples (page 21).

Contemporary with Greenough was Snowden Bell, who began his career as a draftsman under Thatcher Perkins of the Baltimore & Ohio in 1862, later becoming a mechanical engineer and then a patent attorney. His *Early Motive Power of the Baltimore & Ohio* (1912) and many authoritative magazine articles were personally illustrated with the kind of superb drawings that have now become a lost art (page 23).

In many old issues of the *Railway Gazette* one will find various authentic drawings of extinct Pennsylvania and other locomotives by G. H. Caruthers, together with his historical sketches. All such pictorial records are invaluable to the student and collector of railroadiana, and it is fortunate that these and other excellent craftsmen so left their mark for posterity.

Over the years the iron horse has served as the inspiration for many an artist's expedition recorded in volume upon volume of railroad history and description. Hundreds of books on the subject have been published, but most have been photographically illustrated. A few, dependent wholly upon artists for pictorial content, may be mentioned.

Perhaps the earliest illustrated and descriptive railway book was *An Accurate Description of the Liverpool and Manchester Railway* of 1832, which contained several drawings of scenes along its line. One of the first in the United States was Harper's *New York and Erie Rail-road Guide Book* of 1851, which was illustrated with 136 sketches by Lossing and Barritt.

In 1853 Ele Bowen's *Pictorial Sketch-book of Pennsylvania* showed numerous scenes along the Reading Railroad and its affiliated lines. Two years later, his *Rambles in the Path of the Steam Horse*, illustrated by M. Beaulieu, Strother, and Lowrie, similarly described a journey along the main line of the Baltimore & Ohio.

William Sipes's *The Pennsylvania Railroad, Historical & Descriptive,* published in 1875, was profusely illustrated by Thomas Moran, James Hamilton, F. B. Schell, F. O. C. Darley, J. D. Woodward, G. Perkins, W. H. Gibson, and others, the engravings being done by James W. Lauderback.

The Midland Railway, Its Rise and Progress by Frederick S. Williams, published in 1878, was an extra-large book, having over 670 pages with very fine engravings, many by the author.

A large, handsome volume, *Picturesque B & O,* by J. G. Pangborn, appeared in 1882 with illustrations by some of the artists who contributed to the Pennsylvania book, together with C. E. Sickels, Sol Eytinge, W. L. Sheppard, and F. O. Dawson. Their work was translated into steel engravings by the American Bank Note Company, J. Karst, G. Bogert, and others.

An even more elaborate, lavishly illustrated, book by Pangborn was *The World's Rail Way* of 1897. Only about 1,000 were printed, the page size being 11 by 14 inches and containing 300 illustrations, half in color, by the prominent artist E. E. Winchell.

The *American Railway,* a compilation of articles by acknowledged authorities and published by Scribner's in 1889, contained over 200 illustrations by a number of artists.

One more publication in this brief sampling of artistic tributes to the iron horse is deserving of note, even if not so inclusive as the foregoing. The New York Central in 1930 issued *The Run of the Twentieth Century* by Edward Hungerford. This story of one of the world's most famous trains (part of the

1857
One-half inch scale model of the "Phantom"
on display in the Railroad Hall in the Museum
of History and Technology, Smithsonian Institution, Washington, D.C.

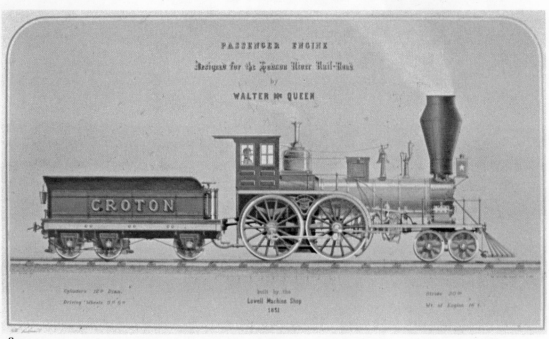

1851

Built for the Hudson River Railroad in 1851, the Croton was designed by Walter McQueen and built by the Lowell Machine Shop. A fine half-inch scale model of this engine is on display at the Smithsonian Institution. This drawing in the style of the old lithographers is the work of Keith Buchanan, and reflects the happy result of accurate research and patient artistry.

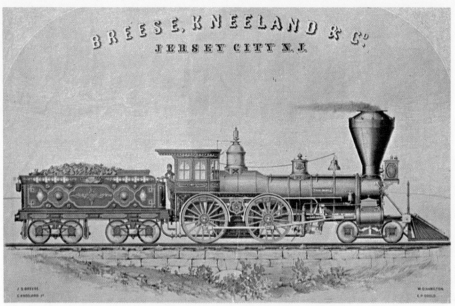

1852–1857

Breese Kneeland & Company had a shop in Jersey City, New Jersey, from 1852 to 1857, where they built locomotives under the name of The New York Locomotive Works. The "Young America" was one of their later engines built for the New York Central Railroad, two others of 1854 being the "Superior" and "Baltic."

Ward Kimball Collection

1908

Baldwin's official photographer, John S. Powell, was also a competent artist, as his watercolors prove. This is a Baldwin-built engine (No. 1421), a compound 4-cylinder express locomotive, for the Great Northern Railway of England. It was painted by Powell in 1908.

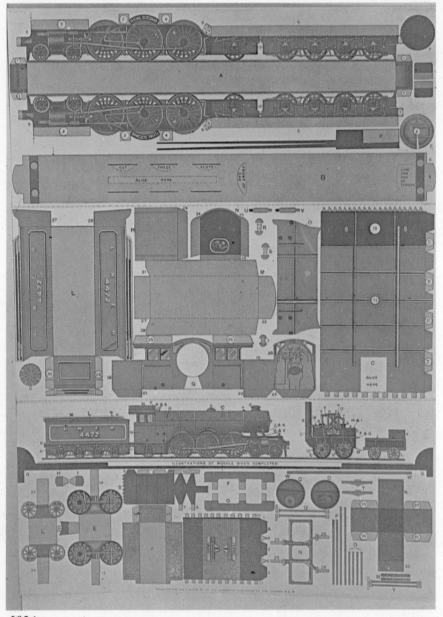

1924

For the British Empire Exhibition of 1924, the London and Northeastern Railway made available these cutout model sheets for "Locomotion No. 1" and the "Flying Scotsman No. 4472" locomotives. They were followed by a matching sheet for the "Experiment" coach of 1825 and the latest sleeping car of 1925.

colloquially known "Steel Fleet") was beautifully illustrated by Frank B. Masters at the time when steam was king on the rails.

In books other than those devoted solely to railroads, one often finds a prominent artist frequently using the theme. For instance, *Our Philadelphia* (1914) by Elizabeth Pennell includes at least ten superb such etchings by her famous brother Joseph.

Another outstanding illustrator was Thornton Oakley, whose works appeared in *Harper's,* among other publications, about fifty years ago, as did other railroad scenes by his contemporary, Jay Hambridge.

1825

One of the earliest locomotive woodcuts from a book by Thomas Gray, London, 1825, shows the locomotive built by Matthew Murray of Leeds for John Blenkinsop and his Middleton collieries, who patented the first rack-rail (cograil) locomotive.

STEAM CONVEYANCE
on a
GENERAL IRON-RAIL-WAY.

No speed with this, can fleetest Horse compare,
No weight like this, canal or Vessel bears,
As this, will Commerce every way promote,
To this, let Sons of Commerce grant their vote.

If the conveyance of Mails across the Channels by Royal Mail Steam-Packets prove so highly important; how much more so, the early distribution of the Foreign & Inland Mails, in all our commercial and manufacturing Districts, by Royal Mail Steam-carriages; the safe and expeditious conveyance of Passengers by Steam-coaches; & the rapid transport of Merchandise of every description, by Steam-caravans and Waggons.

By the Author of Observations on a General Iron-Rail-way.
Published by Baldwin, Cradock & Joy London.

8

awn by N.Whittock.

CHRIST CHURCH AND COAL STAITH, LEEDS.

Engraved on Steel by T. Owen

London. Published by J. T. Hinton, N°4, Warwick Square, March 1829

1825–1830s

These illustrations are three erroneous renderings of early iron horses by artists who had probably never seen one. The first (1825) is from a contemporary print supposedly of a Blenkinsop engine, but providing no footplate for the operator, while the types of cars are quite imaginative. The second shows impossibly high smokestacks and no tender, and the third is allegedly a train in the Mohawk Valley, New York, which does not even remotely resemble the Mohawk & Hudson's "De Witt Clinton."

1829

An early engraving by a prominent British engineer, Charles Vignoles, who in 1823 had surveyed the line for Britain's first railway, the Liverpool & Manchester. The locomotive is the "Novelty," one of the entries in the famous Rainhill Trials of 1829, wherein several locomotives were in competition. The winner was George Stephenson's "Rocket."

1830

On September 15, 1830, the Liverpool & Manchester Railway was opened with much ceremony, and attended by such notables as the Duke of Wellington and Sir Robert Peel. An estimated 50,000 people lined the right of way and crowded the stations. The engines at this opening, according to contemporary information, were the "Phoenix," "North Star," "Rocket," "Dart," "Comet," "Arrow," "Meteor," "Northumberland," and "Planet," the last illustrated from an 1830 print.

RAINHILL BRIDGE.

Published April 18, 1831 by J. F. Cannell, Lord Street, Liverpool

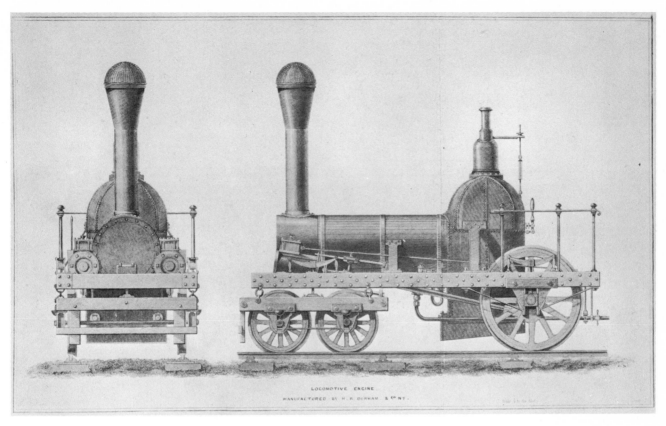

LOCOMOTIVE ENGINE
MANUFACTURED BY H. R. DUNHAM & C.º N.Y.

1849

The Crampton locomotives with their large 7- or 8-foot driving wheels behind the firebox were interesting types, 25 being built for British railways and nearly 300 for German and French lines up to 1864. Robert Stevens, president of the embryo Camden & Amboy Railroad, was impressed by these engines on his trip to England in 1845; and after his return he ordered seven from Richard Norris & Son in 1847. This old lithograph shows one of the slightly varying types that were put into service in 1849.

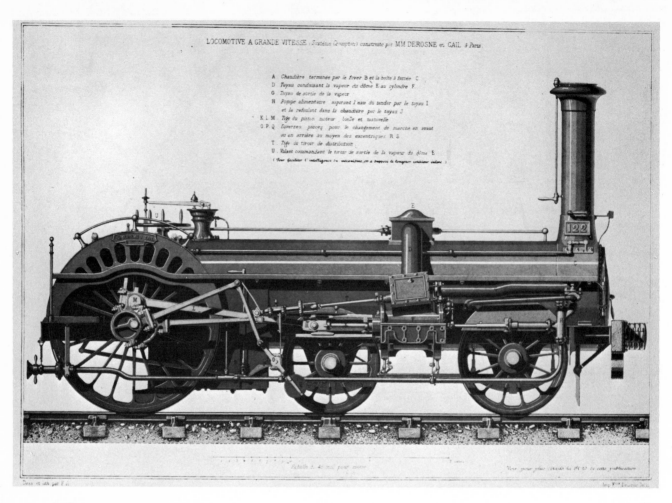

LOCOMOTIVE A GRANDE VITESSE (Système Crampton) construite par MM DEROSNE et CAIL à Paris.

A Chaudière terminée par le foyer B et la boîte à fumée C
D Tuyau conduisant la vapeur du dôme E au cylindre F
G Tuyau de sortie de la vapeur
H Pompe alimentaire aspirant l'eau du tender par le tuyau I
    et la refoulant dans la chaudière par le tuyau J
K L M Tige du piston moteur, bielle et manivelle
O P Q Diverses pièces pour le changement de marche en avant
    ou en arrière au moyen des excentriques R S
T Tige du tiroir de distribution
U Valant commandant le tiroir de sortie de la vapeur du dôme E

1850s

This Crampton type is typical of those used in France in the 1850s, some remaining in service until well into the 1900s. These engines often had difficulty in starting a train, but once under way they were very fast.

1850s

Although locomotives with six driving and no lead wheels were generally designed for switching, this engine, judging by its pilot, or cowcatcher, was evidently used in main-line service. The "Volcano" was built by Rogers in the early 1850s.

1850s

One of the New England factories that branched out into locomotive manufacturing was the Lawrence Machine Shop. This lithograph of the middle 1850s illustrates the "Abbott Lawrence," typical of their workmanship. The small figure on the pilot is quite similar to the familiar ones sold for decorative purposes today.

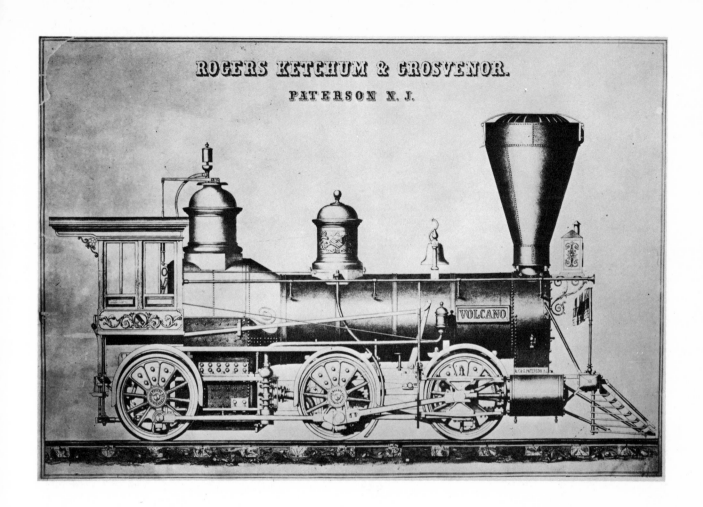

ROGERS KETCHUM & GROSVENOR.

PATERSON N. J.

VOLCANO

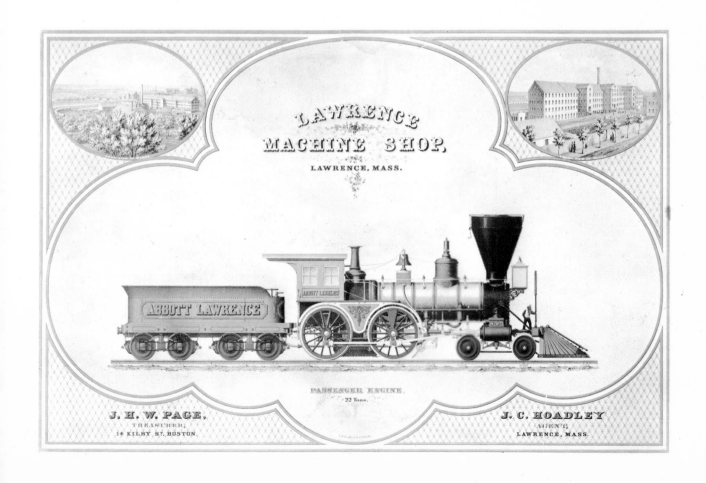

LAWRENCE
MACHINE SHOP.

LAWRENCE, MASS.

ABBOTT LAWRENCE

PASSENGER ENGINE.
22 Tons.

J. H. W. PAGE,
TREASURER,
14 KILBY ST. BOSTON.

J. C. HOADLEY
AGEN'T,
LAWRENCE, MASS.

Manufactured by the TAUNTON LOCOMOTIVE MAN'F'Y CO. H.H. Fairbanks, Agent Taunton, Mass.

1850s

This excellent lithograph of the 1850s shows the "New England," built by the Taunton Locomotive Manufacturing Co., and is typical of the elaborately decorated engines of the time.

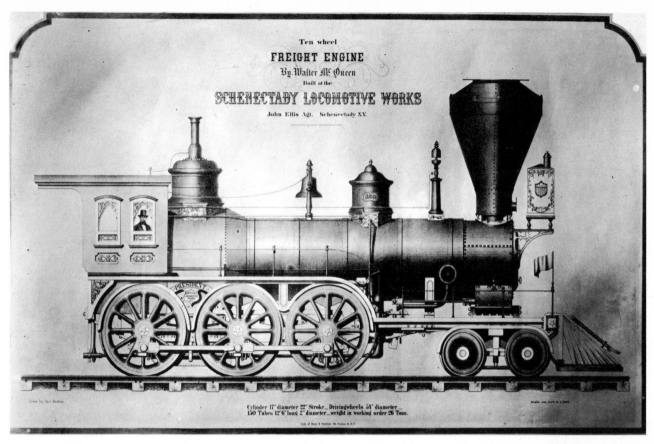

1850s

A Bien & Sterner lithograph for the Schenectady Locomotive Works of a Walter McQueen–designed 10-wheeler, the "President." The figure in the cab is out of proportion to the excellent locomotive drawing.

1851

Built for the Hudson River Railroad in 1851, the Croton was designed by Walter McQueen and built by the Lowell Machine Shop. A fine half-inch scale model of this engine is on display at the Smithsonian Institution. This drawing in the style of the old lithographers is the work of Keith Buchanan, and reflects the happy result of accurate research and patient artistry.

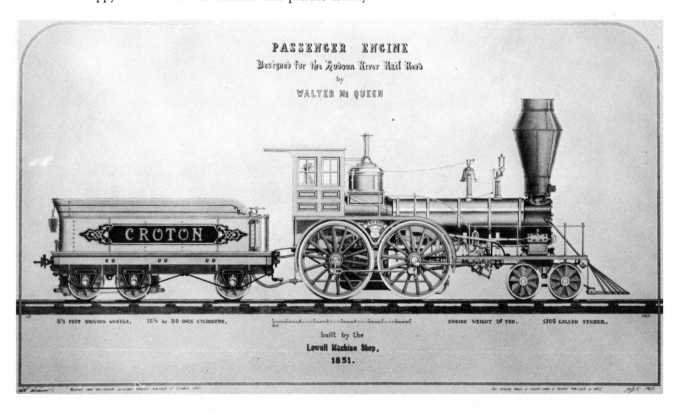

PASSENGER LOCOMOTIVE
LANCASTER (PENN:) LOCOMOTIVE WORKS, N? 1857.
JAMES BLACK, PRESIDENT. JOHN BRANDT SEN? GEN? SUPERINTENDENT. JOHN BRANDT JUN? ASS? SUPERINTENDENT. M.O. KLINE, TREASURER.

1857

A T. Sinclair lithograph of a Lancaster Locomotive Works engine built for the Philadelphia & Columbia Railroad (name reversed in this drawing) in 1857, the same year that, as part of the State System, it became part of the Pennsylvania Railroad. The "John C. Breckenridge" was one of the locomotives designed by John Brandt.

1863

This Currier and Ives lithograph points up the difference between their style of prints and those done for locomotive builders, which were more accurately delineated. The proportions and details of the locomotives shown here are fairly good, the engine on the left being an inside-cylindered type, while that to the right is a more common 4-4-0. Both locomotives are more like types built in the 1850s than like those of the 1863 copyright date.

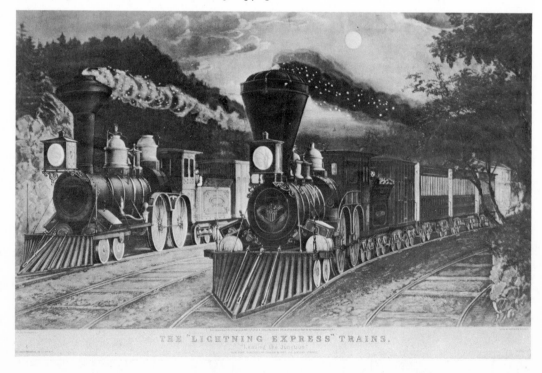

THE "LIGHTNING EXPRESS" TRAINS.
"Leaving the Junction"

1870

This old woodcut from the Oliver Optic Lake Shore Series is believed to be the first to illustrate the rescue of a person from in front of a moving train. "The sparks flew under the drive wheels, but still the iron mass swept on towards the child whose instants appeared to be numbered. It seemed to me that I stopped breathing as the little child disappeared behind the forward part of the locomotive. I expected to hear a shriek—to be conscious that the child was a gory, mangled and shapeless mass beneath. Almost at the same moment, Tom Walton straightened up, holding the child in one arm." *Ward Kimball Collection*

1870s

This Currier & Ives lithograph of the 1870s is perhaps somewhat more accurate than most. But the artist was not too familiar with locomotives, for the smokestacks are too tall, the right-hand engine has an impossible driving-rod arrangement, and the blow-off steam should be coming from the cylinder rather than from under the lead truck. Generally, the detailing is fairly good, although the far too brilliant lighting should be discounted. The early caboose is worthy of note.

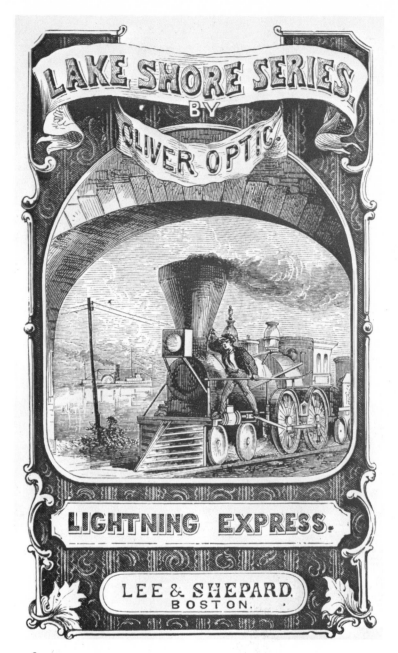

1870

The title page from the Lake Shore Series by Oliver Optic (William T. Adams), Volume 2. The preface reads in part, "Lightning Express, like its predecessor, relates to the Lake Shore Railroad. Waddy Wimpleton and Tommy Toppleton are two characters familiar to all readers. The author has endeavored to keep the moral movement of the story up to the proper standard, and is not afraid that any reasonable young man will like either Tommy or Waddy well enough to imitate their conduct, while he is satisfied that all will be pleased with the moral heroism of Wolf Penniman, and will endorse his views of Christian duty."   *Ward Kimball Collection*

UP IN THE MORNING EARLY.—"THERE WAS NO TIME TO THINK.   IN A FEW SECONDS HE WAS ON THE COW-CATCHER, CLINGING BY ONE HAND,
THE OTHER OUTSTRETCHED TOWARD POLLY."

1880

"There was no time to think. In a few seconds he was on the cow-catcher,
clinging by one hand, the other outstretched toward Polly." So reads the caption
for this engraving from "Up in the Morning Early," a story from Frank Leslie's
Chimney Corner Magazine of September 1880. This is one of the most accurate
illustrations of a locomotive front to appear in connection with this subject.
Ward Kimball Collection

1880s

This is an excellent example of the fine attention paid to detail in an engraving of the 1880s of a typical 4-4-0 locomotive, although no clue as to railroad or location is evident.

1881

Grafton Greenough, later to become one of the executives of the Baldwin Locomotive Works, made this drawing of a locomotive before he joined the company in 1885. He went on to become assistant to Samuel Vauclain, sales manager in 1904, and eventually vice president in 1917.

1882

After many disasters such as shipwrecks, earthquakes, fires, or train wrecks the printmakers were busy commemorating such catastrophes. This print by A. G. D. Folsom and S. C. King was sold after the Ashtabula wreck of 1882.

22

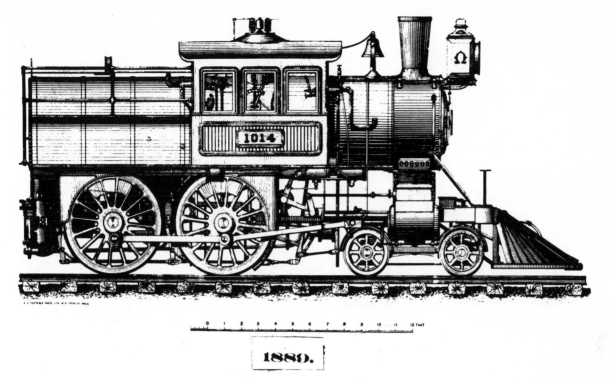

1889.

1889

Snowden Bell was born in Philadelphia in 1843, and as a youth he had two main loves—Baldwin locomotives and Baltimore & Ohio locomotives. He started his career with the B.&O. as a draftsman in 1862 under Thatcher Perkins, Master of Motive Power at the Mount Clair Shops, went with the Pittsburgh Locomotive & Car Works in 1865, and came to Philadelphia in the early 1870s, where he studied at the University of Pennsylvania, graduating with an LLB degree in 1879, and was admitted to the bar that year. He practiced patent law in Pittsburgh until 1909, when he came to New York, continuing to practice there. Most of his work was for Westinghouse Air Brake Co. He was the author of many articles, advocated the Wootten type of locomotive, was considered an authority on boilers, and so on. His book, *Early Motive Power of the Baltimore & Ohio,* is an example, as is this drawing of an Atlantic City Railroad 4-4-0 camelback.

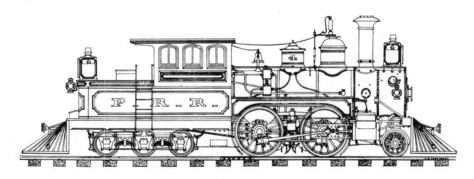

1881

G. H. Caruthers contributed many drawings, such as this, to *Locomotive Engineering* and the *Railway Gazette* in the 1880s and 1890s. Not only was he a most capable draftsman but his familiarity with old locomotives and his personal reminiscences also made his drawings and writings authentic and invaluable additions to locomotive history and research. This is a Pennsylvania Railroad suburban tank engine.

1890s

Earl Chapin May, who was later to collaborate with Samuel Vauclain on his life story, made these water-colors of locomotives when he was nine years old.

PLUCK AND LUCK
COMPLETE STORIES OF ADVENTURE.

No. 12. NEW YORK, June 15, 1898. Price 5 Cents.

ENGINEER STEVE,
THE PRINCE OF THE RAIL.
By Jas. C. Merritt.

There is no stopping now, no turning back! It is all or nothing! Like a flash the engine clears the intervening space, and with an increased impetus leaps the gap! Not the tenth part of a second is occupied in making the awful leap.

PLUCK AND LUCK
COMPLETE STORIES OF ADVENTURE.

No. 235. NEW YORK, DECEMBER 3, 1902. Price 5 Cents.

OLD SIXTY-NINE;
OR, THE PRINCE OF ENGINEERS.
By JAMES C. MERRITT.

As they dashed between the hastily separating Indians there came an awful rush of steam and water as it escaped through the blow-off pipe. Right and left the boiler's scalding contents were sent.

1898–1906

Four cover illustrations for *Pluck and Luck* stories by James C. Merritt, published between 1898 and 1906.
Ward Kimball Collection

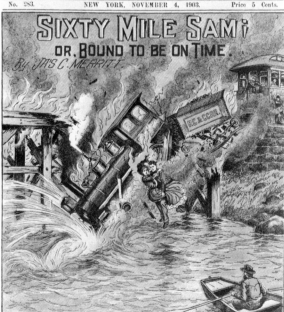

PLUCK AND LUCK
COMPLETE STORIES OF ADVENTURE.

No. 283. NEW YORK, NOVEMBER 4, 1903. Price 5 Cents.

SIXTY MILE SAM;
OR, BOUND TO BE ON TIME.
By JAS. C. MERRITT.

Nellie Borden gave a wild scream and sprang into Sam's arms. Ben Dodge stuck with heroism to his post. One moment the flames overwhelmed the locomotive, blistering the flesh of the occupants, then there was a tremendous rush of waters.

PLUCK AND LUCK
COMPLETE STORIES OF ADVENTURE.

No. 442. NEW YORK, NOVEMBER 21, 1906. Price 5 Cents.

ROB RALSTON'S RUN;
OR, THE PERILOUS CAREER
OF A BOY ENGINEER.
By JAS. C. MERRITT.

The express was in sight when young Rob sprang forward, leaped up into the cart, seized the girl in his arms and jumped. Almost as soon as his feet touched the ground the cart was splintered and the horse instantly slain.

RALPH STEPPED OVER HIS RECUMBENT COMPANION AND PLACED HIS
HAND ON THE LEVER.—P. 42.

Ralph of the Roundhouse.

1905

Allen Chapman wrote a series of railroad stories about Ralph Fairbanks, such as *Ralph of the Roundhouse, Ralph in the Switch Tower, Ralph on the Engine,* and *Ralph on the Overland Express,* in the early 1900s. This is an illustration from the first volume.

1935

On a Sunday afternoon's drive in Connecticut, this old engine, owned by the New Haven Trap Rock Co., was discovered near North Branford. Because so many saplings had grown up around it that a photograph was impossible, A. S. Alexander, the author's father, made this sketch of the Baldwin-built 0-4-0 saddle-tank locomotive of 1886, still intact after nearly half a century.

1886 Baldwin Locomotive
at Branford Conn. April 27/35 — Alex
NORTH

1950s

This scene by George Bradshaw is of a Pennsylvania Railroad train on the Belvidere-Delaware Division in the 1880s. A swing bridge over the Delaware Raritan Canal feeder is in the background.

1930s

A contemporary idea, when the word "streamlining" was new, for modernizing an old steam engine.

1950s

Frank Godwin, of New Hope, Pennsylvania, was the creator of the comic strip "Rusty Riley," as well as a live-steam model locomotive enthusiast (page 164). These are typical of his illustrations depicting the engines he liked so well.

chapter II

The Locomotive in Photography

GENERALLY, PHOTOGRAPHS of the iron horse are divided into two main classes —still pictures and action shots. Collectors of the former are probably the most numerous, while those seeking pictures of trains at speed are likely to be camera as well as engine fans.

Still photos, in turn, are divided into many subclasses, depending upon the individual preference and logical grouping of subjects. One such group might include only builders' photos, those taken by a company's "official" photographer and today available only through other hobbyists or a few dealers. Another might be by individual railroad, an enthusiast specializing in his favorite system's motive power. Period coverage, such as equipment of the 1870s, 1880s, 1890s, or perhaps previous to 1900 or, say, only twentieth-century power would be other logical groupings. Some collectors might want chiefly certain types of engines, such as Pacific, Mogul, or American, to mention only a few of the dozens of possibilities. As an embryo collector becomes familiar with the general subject of steam locomotives, his picture acquisitions sooner or later tend to fall into some form of specialization as the possibilities and variety become apparent.

In still pictures, the most perfect right-side shot of a locomotive with rods at their lowest position is particularly preferred. There must be no object, such as pole, switch stand, or wire, to obscure any details. The lighting must be perfect, preferably when the sun is low so that the shadows will not be too heavy. Collectors of such pictures include camera fans who like to obtain their own shots; but as the iron horse becomes scarcer, recourse is increasingly being had to trading or purchasing prints in all categories.

Among the early railroad photographers must be mentioned the name of the famous Civil War specialist Mathew Brady. Many of his pictures taken for the War Department show United States Military Railroad locomotives, equipment, bridges, and structures. Not all such photos were personally taken by Brady, many being made by his assistants. Other noted photographers who made pictures of the Federal railroads were Captain A. F. Russell and Major General

George H. Barnard. On the Confederate side, George Cook and Milet Rich have left to posterity similar records of southern roads and equipment among their military photographs. The movement of troops and supplies by rail was of major importance to both sides in this conflict, and the photographic record of the part played by the iron horse has a particular fascination for the picture collector and historian of engines. It is interesting to note, thanks to such records, that despite the urgency of the times, considerable pains were often taken to decorate equipment. The tender of the "Gen. Mc Callum" (page 35) is an excellent example of such extravagance.

A few years after the war, the Pennsylvania Railroad had a fairly complete photographic record made of its motive power, and much if not most of this exists today. Although the railroad does not supply prints, many are available. Some of these pictures are of locomotives built many years earlier, and thus constitute a very valuable record of this system's engines from the 1850s into the 1870s.

In the 1870s W. T. Purviance made a series of photographs, many for stereo use of scenes along the Pennsylvania Railroad, then popularly called the "Pennsylvania Central." Some show the famous Horseshoe Curve with only two tracks. Similar stereos were made on many other roads by photographers such as E. W. Beckwith and Charles Weitfle.

Later still, more excellent photographs along rights of way, and sometimes with an occasional locomotive, for publicity and similar uses were made by Rau and Jennings for the Pennsylvania, and Blauvelt and Wortendyke for the New York Central and other roads.

Almost all "official" locomotive builders' photographs were expertly done; they had to be, furnishing as they did a record of engines constructed, and being used for advertising. Some date back into the lithograph era of the 1870s, and include many firms little remembered today—Rhode Island, Richmond, Dickson, Brooks, Schenectady, Cooke, Rogers, and many others, each of whom was turning out distinctive breeds of iron horse. The names of extinct railroads often found on their tenders in these old photographs frequently pose a puzzle for the collector, necessitating research through Moody's and Poor's manuals and official guides of years ago. It might be noted, too, that before the days of reproducing photographs by halftones, the various builders used actual photographs pasted into their locomotive catalogues, which in themselves were often handsome volumes.

In the 1870s, A. F. Bishop, a photographer and artist for the *Scientific American* made some wonderful action pictures of trains, considering the cameras and equipment of that time. The rolling smoke from the locomotive (page 37) shows clearly that there has been no touching up. Most of his photographs were taken along the New York, New Haven & Hartford Railroad.

Many thousands of railroad enthusiasts have taken and are still taking pictures of the iron horse wherever it may be found. Naturally, the emphasis has been on steam, and today little is to be found in the East, and such power is fast disappearing elsewhere as well. Although many prefer to hunt down and record on film whatever they can find in steam locomotives, as with still pictures, an appreciable amount of exchanging and buying goes on, particularly in the field of bygone engines and trains. Although frowned upon by public-relations people, photographs with smoke and steam, if they did not obscure the locomotive, pointed up the action best. Sometimes there were rare opportunities for unusual shots, such as one train passing another, or double- or triple-headers (page 48), and these pictures are particularly interesting and desirable.

Collecting locomotive and railroad photos is not just a recent hobby. Back in the 1890s, Moore's of London (page 41) had a large catalogue of worldwide railways and engines, with hundreds of prints to choose from. Today many a collector and locomotive enthusiast will share copies of his prints with other fans, either by trading or by selling at reasonable prices.

Unfortunately, railroading and its principal actor, the iron horse, have been especially susceptible to errors in representation, not only by artists but also in motion pictures. It is doubtful that there has ever been a movie with trains, old or modern, that has been free of technical errors or anachronisms. Most frequent and glaring were such impossibilities as a Southern Pacific locomotive pulling a train into Boston, New York, or some other eastern city, or perhaps a Pennsylvania engine running between towns nowhere on that system. Then there are the pictures of a train leaving a station with subsequent closeup shots of entirely different power pulling the same train, often even an ancient slide-valve cylindered engine purporting to be the same locomotive. There are also the anachronistic errors of vintage iron horses with air pumps and electric headlights or knuckle couplers, and "foreign" locomotives with headlights and bells. One would think that standard or stock shots of trains properly operating on their own lines would be on file for authentic scenes when required, but evidently few studios cared about authenticity. The argument sometimes advanced to excuse such deviations from accuracy (other than perhaps cost)—that only a purist would know about such details, and they do not matter to the public anyway—is completely specious, and evades the issue.

Like the artists mentioned whose works have helped to perpetuate the memory of the iron horse, some of the photographers of recent years who have done likewise should be similarly credited. For many years Charles Cheney was known for his photographs and intimate knowledge of locomotives. Many collectors recall his shots of eastern roads' motive power, often seen in magazines. His collection of photographs is now preserved at the Smithsonian Institution.

H. W. Pontin has done perhaps more than most photographers to augment the pictorial record of the locomotive with his thousands of photographs taken over many years. Gerald M. Best, too, has taken untold thousands of feet of motion-picture film, as well as still and action shots of motive power, much of it worldwide in scope.

The beautifully composed photographs of William Rittase have captured the atmosphere of railroading in the years before the diesel began to displace steam. His work appeared in *Fortune* and many other magazines.

There are and have been scores of prominent camera fans whose love for the iron horse, perhaps more than their interest in photography, has resulted in priceless records having been made. A few of them are William Osborne, George Doeright, Jr., Joseph Lavelle, D. I. Joslyn, Philip Hastings, Wallace Abbey, Fred Jukes, O. Winston, and Sam Skean.

Among photographic books devoted to this subject are the excellently illustrated *High Iron, Highliners,* and *Mixed Train Daily* by Lucius Beebe. The well-chosen action shots, mostly by Mr. Beebe, but also including some by other outstanding railroad photographers, are particularly fine.

A series of photograph albums, principally by railroads, at popular prices has also been made available to iron-horse lovers.

Photographers of today may find F. W. Blauvelt's remarks of 1897 about taking pictures of fast trains interesting:

> Although photographs have frequently been taken of swiftly moving trains, it is an operation verging very closely on the brink of an impossibility because, to make it successful, so many favorable conditions are necessary at the same instant; one of the first difficulties is to get a proper focus without the sitter (the train) being present, and this is followed by many others too numerous to mention.
>
> The surprising part of this operation is that with the very quick exposure necessary to overcome this motion of the train, enough light can be transmitted through the lens to cause the chemical action on the plate necessary to leave the image upon it.
>
> The exposure on the plates from which photos were made was only 1/130 of a second, which was none too quick, for even in that very small fraction of time a train running 60 miles an hour moves about 8 inches, at 55 miles an hour about 7½ inches and at 53 miles an hour about 7 inches, so that they cannot be successfully taken broadside, and if it were not possible to use a long focus lens which makes a fairly good-sized picture a considerable distance from the object, it is doubtful if an exposure of 1/130 of a second would be quick enough to overcome the motion sufficiently to leave as little blur from it as there is in pictures, even when taken nearly head on.
>
> The rate of speed given is only intended to show as nearly as possible how fast a train was running at the time it was photographed. That of the "Empire State Express" was fixed by the engineer of that train; others were estimated by myself by timing them by the watch for a certain distance as they approached me; this I was enabled to do quite accurately, being perfectly familiar with the localities where the pictures were taken, which were on long stretches of straight track, where I could see the trains coming a mile or more.
>
> The "Empire State Express" runs from New York City to Buffalo, N.Y., 440 miles in 8 hours and 15 minutes (495 minutes), while its rival, the "Black Diamond Express," covers the same distance between

the same points in 9 hours and 55 minutes (595 minutes); this train has very heavy grades to climb which accounts for the time used. The "Royal Blue Line, Limited" runs from New York City to Washington, D.C., 227 miles in 5 hours (300 minutes) and the "Pennsylvania Limited" runs from New York City to Chicago, Ill., 988 miles in 24 hours (1,440 minutes); this train also has very heavy mountain climbing to do. Of course, on all these runs there are several changes of engines, some regular stops and ordinary detention which have to be covered in the time given, and as the three last-mentioned trains start from Jersey City, N.J., a deduction of from 12 to 15 minutes should be made from the running time, for the time used in crossing by ferry boat (1 mile) from New York to and getting away from Jersey City, the schedules all being from New York to various points of destination.

1850s

Here is a Rogers-built 4-4-0 very similar to the famous "General." The "John T. Souter," or No. 17, was a Western & Atlantic engine of antebellum days.   *Wilbur Kurtz*

1860

This is the "Hackensack" as it appeared when new in 1860. Built for the Hackensack & New York Railroad by Rogers, it eventually was relegated to yard service, when the second picture was taken in 1891. Note the absence of headlight, the bell being mounted on its bracket, and the elimination of fancy scrollwork and the pilot.

Very old engine used in Jersey City yards.   *Aug. 17, 1891*

Tender of. Gen. Mc. Callum.

1862

Despite the urgency of the times, the Taunton Locomotive Works spared no effort in decorating the tender of the "Gen. McCallum" for the United States Military Railroads. Most of the many engines built for this service during the Civil War were, of course, much more simply finished.

1864

No. 133, a United States Military Railroads 4-4-0, built by Rogers at City Point, Virginia, in 1864. Note the flowerboxes on the runboard and pilot beam, the occasion for which has not been noted on the old photograph.

1870s

Very few locomotives with vertical boilers were built, the very early Baltimore & Ohio engines being the best-known representatives. This comparatively unknown example was used in maintenance service on the Cumberland Valley Railroad in Pennsylvania in the 1870s, and was probably "homemade" in the company's shop. The crew are (left to right) Hugh Parker, Henry Parker, Charlie Pogue, an unknown, Jos. E. Brambaugh, and John Miller, foreman, Wagonmaker Shop.

1870s

A. F. Bishop, a photographer with *Scientific American,* was probably the first to "stop" moving trains. Previously, engine photographs were all of the still type. This action shot is of a New York, New Haven & Hartford 4-4-0 with a five-car train taken alongside the Quinnipiac River near New Haven.

Cylinders, _18 x 26_ " RHODE ISLAND LOCOMOTIVE WORKS.   Weight, loaded, _70700_ lbs.

Drivers, _62_ " diam.   PROVIDENCE, R. I.   Gauge of Track, _4' 8½_ "

1873

In the 1870s and 1880s most locomotive builders used actual photographs of their productions pasted in their catalogues and on cardboard mounts. Typical of such pictures is this Rhode Island Locomotive Works 4-4-0 built for the New York & Oswego Midland Railroad.

1880s

Ready to leave the original Broad Street Station in Philadelphia (note old train shed), this is No. 98 of the Philadelphia, Wilmington & Baltimore Railroad. This Baldwin built 4-4-0 is handsomely painted and striped, and the crew's pride in the engine is made evident by its polished cleanliness. A note in an old *Locomotive Engineering* appropriately says: "On the P.W.&B. they still have a good many locomotives with red wheels and gold leaf. We know it is out of style and all that but somehow, our heart warms up at the sight of red wheels. Our first love had wheels of warmest red—she also had the coolest firebox we ever saw."

1887

A Shay locomotive built by the Lima Machine Works is illustrated by this old photograph. Mounted on three swiveling trucks, all wheels are gear-driven. This type of engine was built for working grades of 3 to 10 percent, and many were used in logging operations where curves were too short for ordinary motive power. This particular engine weighed 80 tons, and was used on the Sinnemahoning Valley Railroad in Pennsylvania.

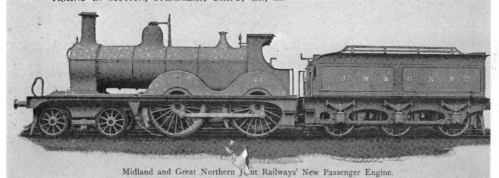
1890

Collecting locomotive pictures is by no means a comparatively recent hobby, as this page from
an English catalogue of 1890 indicates.

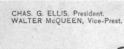

CHAS. G. ELLIS, President.
WALTER McQUEEN, Vice-Prest.

EDWARD ELLIS, Treasurer.
ALBERT J. PITKIN, Supt.

SCHENECTADY LOCOMOTIVE WORKS,

SCHENECTADY, N. Y.

Passenger	Locomotive.	*Ten Wheel Compound*	Type.
Gauge *4 ft. 8½ in.*	Fuel *Bituminous Coal*	Cylinders L.H. *20"* x *24"* R.H. *29"*	Drivers *68"* Dia.
Wheel Base . . .	Driving *12 ft. 2 in.*	Rigid *6 ft. 3 in.*	Total *22 ft. 6 in.*
Weight . . .	On Drivers *97,000*	On Truck *29,800*	Total *126,800*

1890s

No. 284 was a Michigan Central 10-wheel compound engine. Here it is shown in a typical builder's photo of the Schenectady Locomotive Works.

1891

Erie Railroad (New York, Lake Erie & Western) 10-wheeler No. 246 photographed at Jersey City in 1891.

1892

No. 498 of the New York, New Haven & Hartford Railroad was originally No. 9 of the New Haven & Derby line, built by Rogers about twelve years before this 1892 picture was taken.

1893

This is No. 242 of the New York, New Haven & Hartford Railroad as photographed in 1893, a large high-wheeled 4-4-0 built by the Schenectady Works.

1893

An old 1893 photo of Fitchburg Railroad's No. 201. The absence of a pilot would indicate that it was used in freight or switching service.

1893

A Philadelphia & Reading 0-6-0 switcher as it appeared in 1938. With the camelback type of cab and another smaller one forward above the cylinder, No. 42 is unusual.

1893

Several hundred Forney or "double-ender" locomotives were operated on the various elevated railroads in the United States by the 1890s, prior to electrification. This Baldwin compound ran on the South Side Rapid Transit in Chicago in 1893. Note the drip pans under the cylinders and the link and pin couplers.

1893

The record-breaking "999" of the New York Central & Hudson River Railroad is shown here taking water from a "track tank." A system first used in England in the 1860s, the Pennsylvania Railroad adopted it for filling tender tanks in 1870, followed by other American railroads. A trough several hundred feet long between the rails held water into which a scoop was lowered by the fireman on the tender when the engine was running about 45 miles an hour, thus eliminating time-consuming stops at water tanks. The author can recall riding in the first car behind a locomotive when an overflowing tender tank sent a cascade of water into the car vestibule and along the car aisle. *Blauvelt photo*

1894

The "Muley Cow" was the nickname of this engine used in yard service on the Fremont, Elkhorn & Missouri Railroad in the 1890s. Two 6-inch pipes carried smoke and cinders from the distorted smokestack back to the firebox, supposedly reburning them.

1898

First built in 1848, the Baltimore & Ohio's "camels" were a most distinctive class of locomotives, so named because the cans were located on top of the boilers. More than 200 were built, 119 of these for the B.&O., the designer being Ross Winans. This was the last engine of its type in service, the smokestack, headlight, and tender varying from the original appearance.

1900s

A rare photo of a triple-header on the Pennsylvania Main Line near Philadelphia in the 1900s, taken by John Powell. Here are three early H-class Consolidations with a heavy coal train.

1902

The Lehigh Coal & Navigation Company was primarily an anthracite supplier operating many miles of canals in eastern Pennsylvania, supplementing its water-borne traffic by rail from the mines. This is a Baltimore-built 2-8-0 of 1902 as photographed by John Powell.

1902

The Pennsylvania Special, double-headed and westbound near Philadelphia in 1902, is shown in this John Powell photograph. The lead engine is an Atlantic No. 1408, Class E3sd.

1903

This is a perfect example of what the engine picture collector does not want to see . . . the Conneaut, Ohio, enginehouse and yard crew cluttering up a pair of Nickel Plate (N.Y.C.&St.L.) engines in 1903.

1904

The Philadelphia & Reading had a large roster of "camelback" engines, and this is one of their 4-4-0 types used in suburban service. Here No. 152 is waiting at Doylestown, Pennsylvania, at the end of this branch to make the return trip to Philadelphia.

1908

The Pennsylvania Special heading west near Morrisville, Pennsylvania, in 1908 with a K2s Class Pacific.
John Powell

1911

A New York Central Pacific type No. 3590, Alco built, and photographed by John Powell near High Bridge, New York City, in 1911.

1911

Heading toward Baltimore from Philadelphia is this B.&O. express hauled by a Baldwin Pacific No. 5100 in 1911. *John Powell*

1911

One of the crack expresses of the New York, New Haven & Hartford was the Merchants Limited, here shown with an Alco Pacific in the then newly electrified territory west of New Haven. *John Powell*

1920s

The first motion picture to feature the Civil War engine "General," and so named, was made in the late 1920s. Here is Buster Keaton on the pilot of an old locomotive doubling for the "General." The movie was shot on the Oregon Pacific & Eastern Railroad (later the Chambers Lumber Company road). The locomotives were obtained from the Union Pacific, and were originally Oregon Railway & Navigation Co.

1920s

Back in the "silent" days, here Charles Jones is poised for a leap from Engine 2246 in *The Fast Mail,* a William Fox production.

1920s

Another scene from the original "General" movie. Three old engines can be seen in this photograph with Buster Keaton nearest the camera at left.

1923

Baldwin Locomotive Works President Samuel Vauclain's own words describe this picture best: "Not long after our Argentine representative got into action, we turned out the handsomest locomotive in our history. Its jacket bands were polished and nickeled; it had stripes on it here and there; its cabin was finished like a Pullman and it was named the 'President' because it had been selected to haul the new president of the Argentine to his inauguration. We slung its seventy-five tons onto a ship and lashed it there and it arrived at Buenos Aires in good order, all ready to run off the deck and onto rails all steamed up. That was the first time a completely assembled locomotive was shipped from the shores of this country."

1950

George Bradshaw, well known for his etchings of old and historical buildings among many other subjects, designed this copperplate impression of a scene fifty years earlier. This is the former Warren Street Station of the Philadelphia & Reading Railroad in Trenton, New Jersey, with the Revolutionary War Memorial Column in the background. A camelback 4-4-0 locomotive and open-end coaches are ready to leave for the short run to Trenton Junction or West Trenton to connect with Philadelphia or New York expresses.

1870

Comparison of this lithograph with that of the "Young America" will show the lessening of ornate painting and trim in about fifteen years. The builders started in 1841 as Hinkley & Drury, which became Hinkley & Williams and eventually the Hinkley Locomotive Works, continuing in business until 1889 in Boston.

1881

This is the "Emma Nevada" of Ward Kimball's famous 3-foot-gauge San Gabriel Grizzly Flats Railroad. It was built by the Baldwin Locomotive Works in 1881 for the Nevada Central Railroad and was originally named "Sidney Dillon." Renamed "Emma Nevada" after Nevada's famous early-day opera star, it was completely restored over a five-year period to its original appearance. It weighs 22 tons and is a coal burner.

Ward Kimball Collection

1883

"Chloe" (Chloe Kimball's namesake) is Grizzly Flats' Railroad's No. 1. It was acquired from the Waimanalo Sugar Company of Hawaii in 1948 and completely restored, having been built originally by the Baldwin Locomotive Works. The engine's gold leaf and filigree work represent many late hours, blood, sweat, and strained relations in the Kimball household!

Ward Kimball Collection

1927

Harpers Ferry is the center scene on the Baltimore & Ohio dinner plate, one of a set of twenty-one different designs. A series of locomotives from their earliest to latest progress in chronological order around the border.

1850s

One of the very rare porcelain china locomotives made in Germany is this piece named "Eros." Adorned by two cupids at play and another symbol of love stoking the boiler, the "Eros" combined love's sentiment with the mechanical marvel of the age—the steam locomotive. This excellent example of the porcelain maker's art could be used as a flower vase.

Ward Kimball Collection

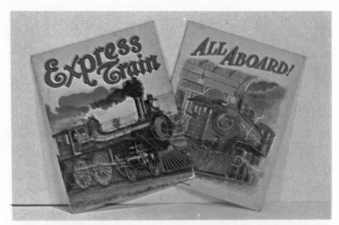

1900s

The cover designs of children's books of the early twentieth century are typically illustrated by these two editions. The artists were not too well acquainted with locomotives or their details.

1880–1914

"Quick as a flash, and with the force of a thunderbolt, Fred knocked the first masked man from the engine, following it up with a lightning stroke that sent the second one after him." Thus Fred Fearnot, along with dozens of other Daring-do heroes, dispatched justice to the hundreds of dastardly villains that slithered their way through the pages of the American dime novel from 1860 to 1910. In purple prose such railroad names as Dan Driver, Tom Throttle, and Switchback Sam captured the fancy of millions of young American boys who dreamed of someday becoming what was considered the most exciting occupation in the world—a locomotive engineer! These are covers of such dime novels.

Ward Kimball Collection

1869—

These are a few of a variety of postage stamps, from the United States and other countries, that featured locomotives. The earliest is the blue United States stamp (at the left of the coin) issued in 1869. The coin is a Mexican silver dollar commemorating the inauguration of rail service.

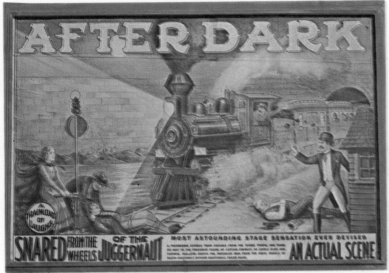

1900s

A theatrical poster about the turn of the century in lurid lithography, reading in part, "A thundering express train crashes from the tunnel portal and tears its way to the prostrate figure of Captain Chumley, as lovely Eliza and faithful old Tom snatch the imperiled man from the cruel jaws of death—dastardly Richard Knatchbull foiled again."

Ward Kimball Collection

1900s

Almost from the beginning, the American circus relied heavily on the railroad and on the power of the steam locomotive for transportation. Many advance circus posters, like that of the Sells Brothers shown here, featured locomotives and their circus trains to extoll the thrills and gigantic size of the "Greatest Show on Earth."

Ward Kimball Collection

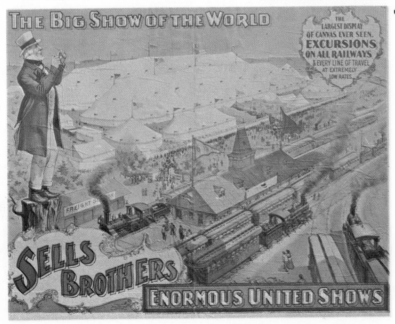

1870–1895

Here is a fine sampling of the locomotives of wood and tin floor or pull trains from the Ward Kimball Collection. The wooden locomotives and cars had brightly colored paper glued over their shapes, most being made by Milton Bradley of Springfield and W. S. Reed Company of Leominster, Massachusetts. The painted tin engines and cars had stenciled lettering and designs.

1883

This is a Fallows tin train of the early 1880s. Such old toy trains in very good condition are becoming quite rare.

Ward Kimball Collection

1875

The H. S. Reed Company made wood and paper trains—some quite large. This "Jack and Jill" locomotive is 18 inches long, and the passenger car 21 inches.

Ward Kimball Collection

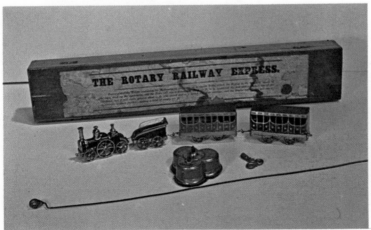

1850s

Probably the earliest of toy trains driven by a clockwork mechanism is the "Rotary Railway Express," the approximate date of the 1850s being deduced by the type of locomotive and the stagecoach type of cars. In operation, the clockwork mechanism is wound up, set on a table, the wire attached, and the locomotive and its train hooked on to its other end, whereupon it travels in a circle. This is one of the rarest of all early toy trains.

Author's Collection

1903–1911

Among clockwork locomotives, these early Ives examples are choice collectors' items. At upper left is a 1903 engine, and to its right a larger 4-4-0 of 1904, both o gauge. Below is a handsome No. 40 with the first car of its train in 1 gauge.

Ward Kimball Collection

1905

Dating from 1859, the name Marklin is one of the most famous among toy and train manufacturers. The company is still very much in business in Göppingen, Germany. This is a typical 1905 o-gauge train with some of the infinite number of accessories the firm produced.

Ward Kimball Collection

1910

J. A. Issamayer is one of the lesser-known toy-train manufacturers. This is one of their clockwork o-gauge locomotives and train made for the American market.

Ward Kimball Collection

1916

Most of the cast-iron clockwork locomotives made in Germany were produced by Bing, although an occasional Bub or Marklin turns up. This 4-4-0, station, and cars by Bing are similar to their counterparts made in this country by Ives.

Ward Kimball Collection

1875–1890s

These are brass live steamers, alcohol or spirit fired. Above are Stevens Model Dockyard engines of the 1890s, and below are earlier French-made locomotives of about 1875.

Ward Kimball Collection

1885–1890

A very rare Jean Schoenner Company's 4-inch-gauge locomotive from 1885 is shown above in this illustration. It is 25 inches long. Below are 1-gauge engines made by Bing.
Ward Kimball Collection

1902–1908

Two 3-gauge toy steam locomotives, the "King Edward" from 1902 and the "Charles Dickens" of 1908, made by Bing. The former was seen briefly on a shelf in the nursery sequence of the Walt Disney production *Mary Poppins*.
Ward Kimball Collection

1906

Carlisle & Finch made this electrically driven Atlantic-type engine for 2-rail 2-inch gauge in 1906.

Ward Kimball Collection

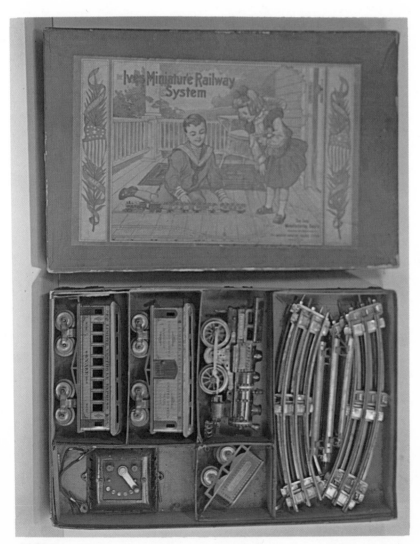

1912

Discovering an original almost new and scarce set of trains in its original box is one of the joys of collecting old toy trains. Here is such a set—an Ives train with a No. 1117 locomotive of 1912. The penciled price on the end label is $7.50!

1931

One of the very popular trains among toy-train collectors is the Lionel "Blue Comet," a standard-gauge set first catalogued in 1930 with a No. 390E 2-4-2 locomotive. In the following year, and until last listed in 1938, it consisted of the No. 400 4-4-4 engine illustrated and three matching passenger cars.

1922–1939

Appropriately enough, the steam locomotive, prototype or toy, was pictured on many covers of toy-train catalogues, being followed eventually by electric engines. These are typical catalogues from the 1922 Voltamp to 1939 Marklin, the others including Lionel, Ives, Dorfan, Bing, and Bassett-Lowke.

1856

This is a ⅜-inch scale model of the Pennsylvania Railroad's "Tiger," a fast passenger engine of 1856. The prototype was one of four similar engines (others were "Leopard," "Hornet," and "Wasp") built by the Baldwin Works, and represented the highest development of American passenger locomotives up to that time. The model, together with the "John Bull" and "Black Hawk," was built for part of the décor of a Savarin restaurant in 1938.

Alexander

1859

A model of the Civil War period, this ½-inch scale replica is on display at Fort Donelson Military Park. Moore & Richardson of Cincinnati built the prototype for the Louisville & Nashville Railroad in 1859. The model was made in 1961.

Alexander

1960s

These HO model locomotives were custom-finished by Dom Ferraro—fine examples of how standard models can be improved by proper painting and lettering. They comprise in order of prototype dates an inspection engine of the late 1880s, a Prairie (2-6-2) of the early 1900s, a Baltimore & Ohio "President Grant" P7 Pacific type of 1927, a Southern Railroad Ps4 Pacific of 1929, two Southern Pacific GS class "Daylight" locomotives of 1937, a Canadian Pacific 2-10-4 Selkirk T-1c class of the late 1940s, and a Duluth Missabe & Iron Range 2-8-8-4 M4 class articulated.

1830s

An unusual and rare inkstand with a typical British locomotive, following the 2-2-2 type of Stephenson, Hawthorn, or Tayleur, with inside cylinders. The finish is gold and silver, and the scale of the engine about ¼ inch to the foot.

Author's Collection

1850s

This is one of the early series of jigsaw puzzles where, unlike the intricate cutouts of today, the separations were made in straight lines. This 8-by-24-inch lithograph was also instructive in naming the principal parts of the locomotive.

Ward Kimball Collection

1870

Locomotive weathervanes are not too common, especially old ones. This 3½-foot engine is most unusual in that it is not a flat cutout or even in bas-relief, but is a full three-dimensional model. It was made by Cushing & White of Waltham, Massachusetts, about 1870, and has copper, iron, and zinc components.

Ward Kimball Collection

1899

Featured in the John Wanamaker Christmas catalogue of 1899, this puzzle is typical of the period, with fancier cutouts than the 1850 type. It is 18 by 24 inches in size.

Ward Kimball Collection

1900s

Featuring English and American trains, this jigsaw puzzle set consisted of four scenes. A duplicate colored picture of each puzzle was included as a guide, as the upper and lower right-hand illustrations show. This set was made in Germany.

1929

To commemorate the centennial of the first running of the "Stourbridge Lion" on the Delaware & Hudson Railroad, this medal was struck in 1929. Various other medals bearing locomotive likenesses have marked historic occasions of railroad history.

1926

Chicago suburban service on the Illinois Central employed locomotives such as this somewhat modernized 2-4-4 tank of the late 1880s. Electrification in 1926 spelled the end of steam operation.

1927

Typical of commuter service to New Jersey shore points is this Central Railroad of New Jersey Atlantic No. 805 photographed at Lakehurst in 1927 by William Osborne.

1927

The Canadian Pacific's "Dominion" double-headed eastbound over Kicking Horse Bridge.
Powell Collection

1927

A double-header on the Canadian Pacific in the Canadian Rockies.   *Powell Collection*

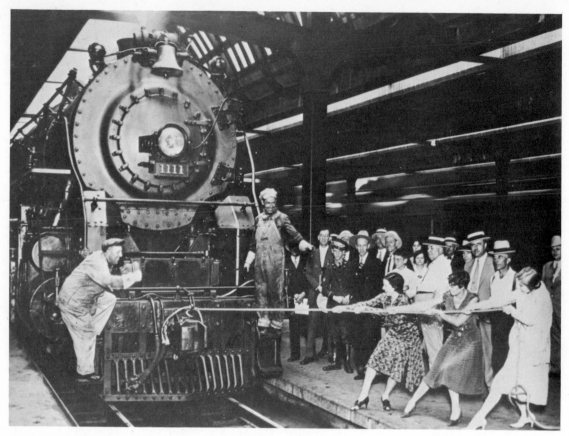

1930

The first locomotive to be designed and equipped with roller bearings was the Timken No. 1111, or "Four Aces," built by Alco in 1930. It was demonstrated on 14 different railroads, and after having traveled some 89,000 miles, went to the Northern Pacific in 1933. This publicity picture supposedly showed the easy rolling properties of roller bearings.

1930s

The Rahway Valley Railroad operates about nine miles of freight service from Roselle Park to Summit, New Jersey. This was one of their Consolidation type locomotives (formerly Lehigh & New England) in the 1930s, before dieselization.

1930

A special paint job was often done by locomotive builders for the photographic record, after which a standard finish was applied. This example in flat gray with white rods and wheel rims is an Erie C-3-A Class 8-wheel switcher built by Baldwin in 1930.

1930

This Hudson type No. 4000 Class S-4A on the Burlington Lines was roller-bearing equipped on all crankpins and axles. In 1936 it was streamlined and named "Aeolus."

1932

The Chesapeake & Ohio in April of 1932 inaugurated a new deluxe, completely air-conditioned train between Washington and Cincinnati, with cars originating in New York and Indianapolis. F19 Class Pacifics were assigned to this service, and this is a head-on view. A model of the "George Washington" ran on the C.&O.'s 80-foot-long model railroad at the Century of Progress Exhibition in Chicago in 1933.

1933

When the London, Midland & Scottish Railway sent the Royal Scot train to the Century of Progress Exhibition at Chicago, it was also posed for many pictures en route. This unusual photograph shows this distinguished visitor alongside one of the famous K4 Pacifics of the Pennsylvania Railroad.

1939

One of the "epic" movies was *Union Pacific,* a Paramount picture produced and directed by Cecil B. De Mille in 1939. This is one of the trains with No. 58, a 4-4-0, at the head end.

1935

A night scene in the Pennsylvania Railroad's Philadephia yards, showing a group of six passenger locomotives.

1939

This 2-4-0 was used in some sequences in the picture *Union Pacific,* which included in the cast Barbara Stanwyck, Joel McCrea, Akim Tamiroff, Robert Preston, Lynne Overman, and Brian Donlevy.

William Kimball Collection

1939

The Missouri Pacific acquired this U.S.R.A. engine in 1919. In 1939 they rebuilt it at their Sedalia Shops with modern features such as Baldwin "Box-Pok" driving wheels and modern pilot.

1940

Dodge City was another popular movie with a railroad theme. This Warner Bros. production featured Errol Flynn, Olivia De Havilland, and Ann Sheridan.   *William Kimball Collection*

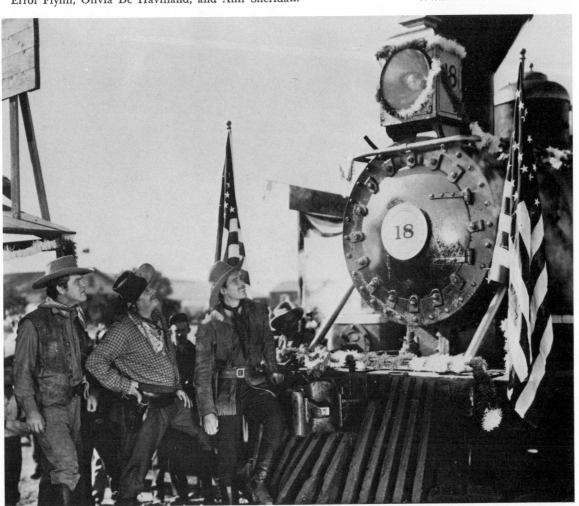

1940s

The *Harvey Girls,* an M-G-M production, used the old Virginia & Truckee No. 18 in some sequences. Here is Ray Bolger on its running board.   *William Kimball Collection*

1956

Featuring the Baltimore & Ohio's famous "Wm. Mason" as the "General," Walt Disney's *Great Locomotive Chase* starred Fess Parker and Jeffrey Hunter, shown here in the production released on June 8, 1956. *William Kimball Collection*

1944

This detail close-up of a 2-6-6-4 locomotive is a perfect example of excellent photography, as any camera fan would agree. Built by Lima, this was one of the last steam engines made for the Chesapeake & Ohio.

chapter III

The Locomotive in Glass and China

PROBABLY THE EARLIEST form of glass showing anything pertaining to the railroad is the whiskey bottle made to commemorate the groundbreaking of the Baltimore & Ohio Railroad in 1830. While not showing the iron horse, it did have a horse drawing a wagon on rails molded in the design, and "Success to the Rail Road" as the inscription. Some originals are to be found today, although a number of reproductions from the old molds have been made in recent years.

The Boston & Sandwich Glass Co., founded by Deming Jarves in 1825, was one of the best-known firms making most kinds of glass, although pressed glass is most often associated with the name "Sandwich." Probably the most accurate or faithful likeness of a locomotive in this medium is a plate of 1875 depicting the first mail train on the New York Central. This is one of the few Sandwich pieces where the date of manufacture is evidence (page 72).

There were other pressed-glass pieces commemorating various dates and affairs relating to railroads, even cartoons, most having been made in the 1870s. Later came the candy containers and other three-dimensional forms of the iron horse.

In recent years manufacturers have etched and otherwise applied locomotive designs on many utilitarian glass items. Various drinking glasses, flasks, and other bottles bear these likenesses. Many, unfortunately for the purist, have stylized or otherwise distorted pictures of engines. Some have been and are being made for dining- or club-car use by a number of railroads, and are usually available from them.

Very few pieces of old china reflected the iron horse. There were a limited number of exceptions, such as Enoch Wood's Staffordshire plates with primitive English designs, but this old theme has been much more recently revived, and is found in modern china. Even some Currier & Ives railroad scenes have been reproduced in color on English-made china.

The largest quantity of china and the greatest variety of designs pertaining to the locomotive or railroads are to be found in that made for dining-car service. Each railroad has, of course, had its own designs, although few actually used the locomotive theme. Outstanding in this category of china was that of the Baltimore & Ohio Railroad.

On the occasion of their centennial in 1927, the Baltimore & Ohio held the "Fair of the Iron Horse" at Halethorpe, Maryland, near Baltimore. Many of their historic, as well as modern, locomotives and cars were on display and were demonstrated, as were some from other railroads, and the fair was an outstanding event in railroad history.

Timed to coincide with their centennial, a set of china was designed and made for their dining-car service totaling some twenty-one different pieces. The idea was generated by the original two Staffordshire plates made in 1827 at Burslem, England, which had on their reverse "The Baltimore & Ohio Rail Road," although the English potters did not depict American locomotives.

For the B. & O. set a series of locomotives, from their earliest "Tom Thumb" to the latest "Lord Baltimore," followed each other in sequence around the borders of each piece, and their centers depicted scenes along the main line, such as Harpers Ferry and Cumberland Narrows (page 76).

The Scammell China Company of Trenton, New Jersey, was given the order. Founded in 1869 as the Lamberton Works, it became part of the Maddock China Company in 1892. In 1901, D. William Scammell joined the firm, and in 1922 acquired the controlling interest and formed the Scammell China Company.

This special B.&O. china was two years in the planning and making. The copperplate engravings were entirely done by hand, the designers and artists being Frank Guilford and Tony Draggonnetti. The number of dots to show shading and detail was approximately 2,600 per square inch, the dinner plate (Harpers Ferry) having more than 90,000 in the varying depth required. Never before in American pottery had such a large amount of copperplate been required for a single set of china. The original pieces of the 1927 series had a plaque on the reverse of the larger pieces, while those subsequently made had merely "Lamberton China." Scammell probably made more dining-car china than any other American maker through the 1930s. Some of the railroads supplied were the Pennsylvania, Union Pacific, Lehigh Valley, Norfolk & Western, Atlantic Coast Line, New Haven, and Seaboard Air Line.

1830s–1860

Two ornate china inkwells, dating probably to the 1830s, and a later glass type.   *Winey Collection*

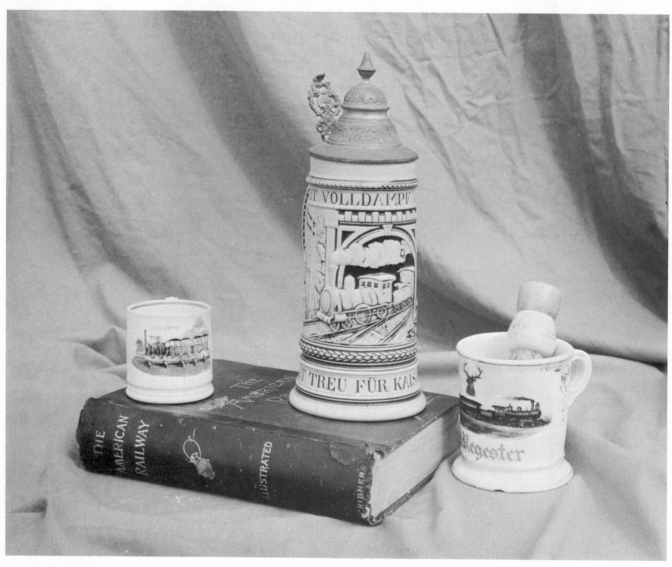

1830–1880s

Three china pieces with the locomotive theme. At left, a teacup from the 1830s with a Blenkinsop type of locomotive. In the center a German stein; translated, the inscription reads "With full steam ahead for king and country." At right is an occupational shaving mug of the 1880s, with the owner's name, "William Regester," in gold.

William Kimball Collection

1860s

A most unusual and rare tea server, which once belonged to Jefferson Davis and which may be seen at the Smithsonian Institution.

1875

A Sandwich glass plate made to commemorate the first "Fast Mail" on the New York Central & Hudson River and Lake Shore railroads. On September 16, 1875, the run from New York to Buffalo was made in 11 hours and 15 minutes at an average speed of 50 miles an hour.

1880s

A pressed-glass "Knights of Labor" plate with a locomotive and ship shown in the border.

72

1880s

A pressed-glass "cartoon" plate showing a train, and the prelude to an accident.

1890, 1950s

At upper left is an old-time engineer's shaving mug. At upper right is a coffee cup, and in the center a plate, both transfer-decorated.   *A. Schrader*

1890

This is the firescreen from the Board Room of the old Baldwin Locomotive Works when they were at Broad and Spring Garden streets in Philadelphia. The center panel shows a hand-painted Central Railroad of New Jersey 4-4-0 engine. Several hundred pieces of glass are leaded into the rest of the screen, which is about 3 feet long.

These are three locomotive candy containers, the longest being about 5 inches. The smallest, at the top, was found in the ruins of a Bucks County, Pennsylvania, farmhouse.

1927–1930s

At the top is an Italian tile, and at upper left and center are commemorative plates. The center plate is from the New Haven's dining-car service, and the other pieces are Baltimore & Ohio dining-car china.

1950s

This English china of recent manufacture is transfer-decorated in the old style with primitive locomotives and cars.

1950s

An apothecary-type bottle depicting several old locomotives.

1955

Three of a set of six different plates hand painted on deep bas-relief.
Designed by the author

1950s

Locomotives in china: a planter, a catchall dish, and two ashtrays.

77

chapter IV

The Locomotive in Design

MOST LIKENESSES OF THE IRON HORSE that have been included in this category are engravings—beautiful examples of this highly specialized craft. Most early stocks and bonds issued by railroad companies had the theme of the locomotive appropriately woven into their designs. Though innumerable variations of the subject were done, except in rare instances they did not depict equipment of the particular railroad, but rather composite or representative types of engines.

Some railroad passes also depicted the iron horse and are shown on page 84, although most were not so ornate, bearing the title of the railroad, conditions, and space for recipient's name. Except for a few souvenir tickets, engravings of locomotives were seldom used in this type of printing. Many years ago, for other miscellaneous printing, job shops had standard cuts of separate locomotives and cars that could be set up to make a train. Many of these still exist.

The influence of the iron horse through the last century and into modern times is occasionally expressed by means of postage stamps. It is surprising that the United States has printed very few such stamps. The earliest stamps with a locomotive was a three-cent blue of 1869; then came a two-cent red and black of 1901 (Empire State Express), and next a five-cent red parcel post stamp of 1912, the only ones to appear until recent years. Most South American countries had engines on their stamps at some time or other. Only in recent times, and somewhat belatedly, has a bit more attention been accorded the subject, such as Egypt's Railway Congress issue of 1933 (four stamps), Belgium's 1934 set of three, and 1935 set of twenty-four, Germany's 1935 set of four and France's 1937 set of two. For a specialized collection of railway stamps only, including all the denominations in sets, there is probably a potential of several hundred.

The likeness of the iron horse can be seen on many private or semigovernment issues of old paper money or bank notes. The finely detailed engravings, like those of stock certificates, are well worth the collector's attention. In number there are probably almost as many varieties to be discovered as in stamps (pages 82 and 83).

Christmas and other greeting cards would seem to come under the heading of design, and here the possibilities and diversity for collectors are endless. Though the majority of them are very ornate and fancifully colored, they are almost caricatures of the iron horse. Nevertheless, despite the artistic license, the theme pleases the enthusiast. A fair proportion of cards are generally accurate in their depiction of steam engines, which seem to be principally of the 1870s. There are some more modern renderings, too, but very few thus far seen, perhaps fortunately, have diesels for their theme.

Even fabrics reflect the iron horse, two old designs being shown on pages 176 and 177. In more recent years material for curtains or drapes has had patterns of locomotives; and in clothing, shirts, neckties, and handkerchiefs enable a railroad enthusiast to indulge his interest.

Paper products, such as napkins, coasters, and wrapping papers, also bore this theme. Wallpaper, too, has depicted railroad and locomotive scenes, and some has been especially designed as backgrounds for model railroads.

Through the formative years of the iron horse, innumerable ideas and designs were conceived to improve the breed. Most of these were supposed to increase efficiency or power or to economize on fuel. So many of them—a large proportion bordering upon fantasy—came to the desk of the editor of *Locomotive Engineering* that in 1897 the publication presented the "ultimate" in locomotive design. Because of its satirical humor a few of the many gadgets featured are described here, and refer to the illustration on page 86:

THE ELI GILDERFLUKE PERFECTED LOCOMOTIVE

. . . 7 is an especially designed 19 inch air brake pump, which together with a new and improved brake rigging, will stop a train of 70 cars at a speed of 42.7 miles per hour, in 8 feet, 10 inches. This will enable an engineer to run at full speed right up to the station platform, thus saving many money-bearing minutes, now lost by the slowing up of trains entering stations or terminals.

8 and 9 are air brake pump steam exhaust and supply pipes, in the order named, the supply being taken from the dry pipe to the front cylinder of the lower tandem-compound portion of the engine.

10 is a new and vastly improved smoke pipe or carbowallop for the swift conveyance of smoke, cinders and gases back to the fire box for re-incineration, and with a nice new lead pencil and a sheet of smooth brown paper, a saving of at least 75 per cent in coal consumption can be easily figured, and in actual service there is no doubt but what a train of 68 cars and a short caboose can be hauled 137.49 miles per half ton of coal.

52, 53, 54, 56, 57 pertain to sundry and divers driving and traction wheels, all designed to one end—that of the highest speed, combined with a great economy and perfect safety. By the use of these traction and driving wheels great tractive power is obtained, the pull on the drawbar representing 213,547 pounds. Theoretically, this engine will easily haul 294 standard freight cars of 60,000 pounds capacity, fully loaded at a speed of 84 miles an hour. . . . at a speed of 119 miles per hour, this engine will make no more noise in operation that a yellow tom cat crossing a wooden bridge.

86, 87, 91, 92 are portions of the cinder hopper or frugoeconomiter, and is a device for separating the coal and cinders coming through the carbowallop and delivering them on a shelf at the back end of fire box, where the fireman with a pair of asbestos mittens removes large rocks, bits of wire and scrap tin before returning the coal or cinders to the firebox. Should the frugoeconomiter become choked by material too large to pass through to the firebox, the fireman can remove the covers 87, 91 and hit the conjested mass a t'ump with an eight pound hammer provided for the purpose, thus starting the stuff in the direction intended by the inventor. This device exerts a coal saving of 25 per cent, which, combined with the saving effected by the carbowallop, makes a coal economy of 120 per cent. The improvements now making will result in these engines becoming coal producers instead of coal consumers, and doubtless the railroads adopting this locomotive will have coal for sale or to give away.

The topic thus far has been the *idea* of the iron horse as used in and for design, rather than the plan of the machine itself. This came about as a logical development through the years as trains became heavier and more speed was demanded, with locomotive designers meeting the challenge. However, emphasis was on power and efficiency, with little attempt to give locomotives "eye appeal"; although iron-horse lovers will claim they needed nothing more. In the middle 1930s a number of attempts at streamlining were made. There were the New York Central Hudsons designed by Henry Dreyfuss, with several variations of "bullet nose" and other forms. The Pennsylvania had Raymond Lowey streamlined K4 No. 3768, perhaps the apex for eye appeal in this field. The Baltimore & Ohio had several types, and the Milwaukee Road's "Hiawatha" was also a milestone. The New Haven's Hudsons built by Baldwin are worthy of note, and a number of semistreamlined engines appeared on the Southern Pacific, the Santa Fe, and British, Continental, and other roads. All these locomotives were used in passenger service, but the thin smoke of the diesel was already tracing its mark on the wall, and the trend was not extended.

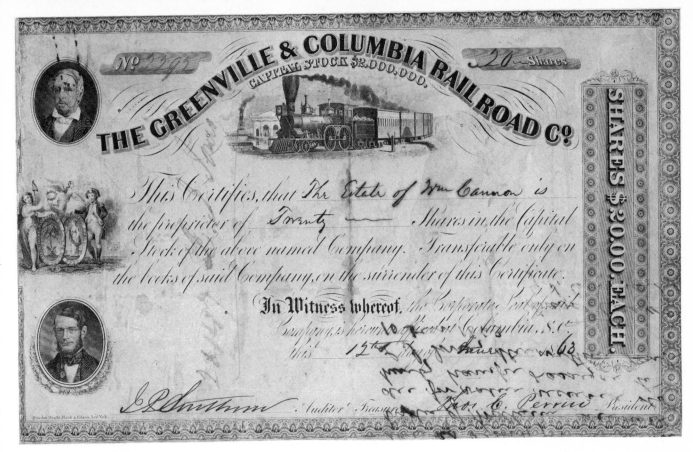

1863

The Greenville & Columbia Railroad Co. issued this stock certificate in 1863. This railroad is now the Lancaster & Chester.

1871

A fine example of the American Bank Note Company's engravings, enlarged. This is probably a station in New England. The detail is excellent, and the locomotive is authentic but unidentifiable except for "Rogers" on the cylinder.

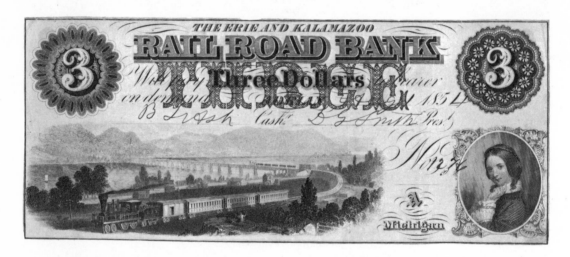

1840–1862

In currency bearing engravings of locomotives, the engines shown were usually "stock" or standard likenesses. The $3.00 note shown, although for an Adrian, Michigan, bank, depicts the Pennsylvania Railroad's first bridge across the Susquehanna River, above Harrisburg, being crossed by an unlikely-looking locomotive and train.

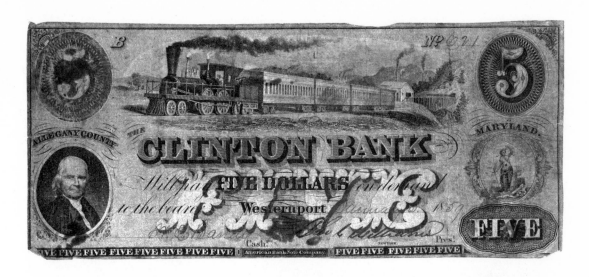

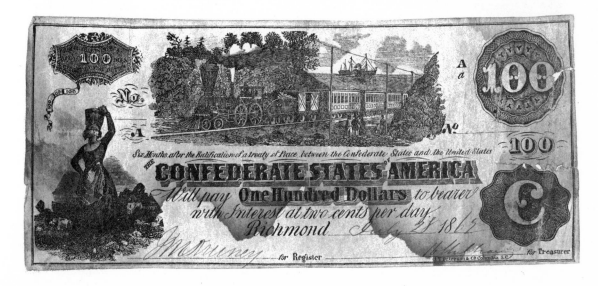

1874–1936

Railroad passes by the hundreds of thousands have been issued, basically for the transportation of employees. Three early ones of the 1870s are shown here. "The Royal Blue" train ticket and that below for the Fair of the Iron Horse were among the very few souvenir tickets to be issued. The lower-right-hand coupon was issued by the Pennsylvania Railroad in the 1920s to ticket holders for the "Broadway Limited." If the train was more than 55 minutes late, a partial refund was made based on this lateness. The New York Central accorded patrons of the "20th Century Limited" similar consideration.

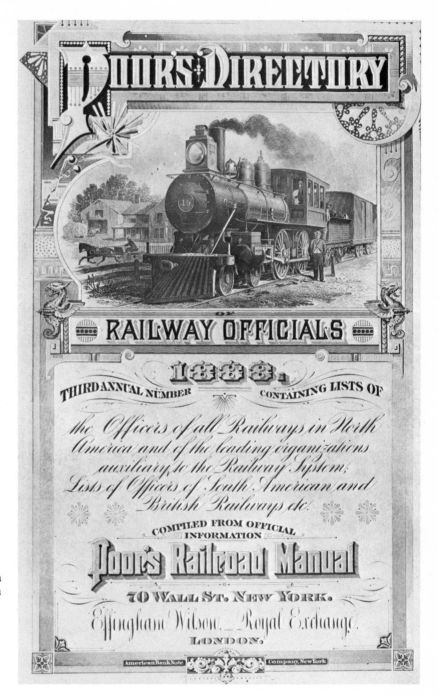

1888

A beautifully engraved title page from *Poor's Directory* of 1888 by the American Bank Note Company.

1897

An imaginative and satirical drawing of a suggested locomotive that would be the ultimate in efficiency, this "Gilderfluke" illustration is from *Locomotive Engineering*. Excerpts from the original description appear in the text.

1905

Many thousands of stock certificates incorporated locomotives in their designs. Here is one of the Missouri, Kansas & Texas Railway with a locomotive as well as a fireman.

86

As part of the Ives company's advertising, a set of stamps depicting locomotives was designed, and these are a few examples.

1850s–1930s

A sampling of a few of the many thousands of brochures and other printed matter distributed by the railroads through some eighty years. Booklets featuring summer excursions and extolling vacation spots were plentiful in the 1900s. Others described crack trains, engineering accomplishments, or other achievements.

1936

The Pennsylvania Railroad commissioned Raymond Loewy to streamline one of the famous K4 Pacifics, and here is No. 3768 after its conversion. The GG-1 electric locomotives were also Loewy-designed.

1937

Reminiscent of ancient helmets are these front ends of New York Central J3a Hudsons designed by Henry Dreyfuss in 1937. They were used on the "20th Century Limited" and other fast passenger trains.

1937

A streamlined Santa Fe Hudson No. 3460 entering Chicago with the "Chief" in 1937.

1937

A Baldwin version of streamline design was this Hudson type for the New Haven Railroad in 1937. These 1400-Class locomotives were used on Shore Line trains between New Haven and Boston.

1937

Early in 1937, six GS-2s locomotives, the first streamlined type on the Southern Pacific, were placed in service. Built by Lima, they were later followed by the somewhat more powerful GS-4s, one of which, No. 4439, is illustrated. See color section for models of these engines.

chapter V

The Locomotive in Advertising

THE BUILDERS OF THE MACHINES were probably the first to use artist's renderings of the iron horse commercially. While the earlier engravings were mostly for book and engineering use, the advent of many firms, especially those already making machinery, into the manufacture of locomotives spurred competition, and soon all were having likenesses of their products put on stone, and issuing advertising lithographs. Through the late 1840s, 1850s, and 1860s, many beautiful examples of lithographers' craftmanship preserve in excellent detail the contemporary engines in their handsome colors and trim. Like the coachmakers, the painters went "all out" in decorating locomotives, even to scenes or portraits on headlights, cabs, and panels of tenders. Polished brass and copper lavishly applied constituted the brightwork. The finished products were truly works of art, results of a happy collaboration of designers, builders, and finishers. Even though the decoration was gradually dispensed with through the 1870s, until almost 1900 much attention was still paid to elegant finish and trim, even if the brilliant colors had disappeared. Note, for instances, a few of the specifications of James Buchanan for his famous "999" of 1893:

> Boiler to be lagged with asbestos cement and jacketed with Russia iron, secured by Russia iron bands. Lagging and jacket to extend over smoke box and in cab to end of boiler.
> Cab—Cab substantially built of black walnut secured with joint bolts and corner irons. Ceiling of alternate ash and black walnut strips. To be finished with seats and tool boxes for engineer and fireman. Sash to be fitted with plate glass. Woodwork to be well rubbed, oiled and varnished.
> Painting—Engine and tender to be painted black and varnished, each coat of paint to be well rubbed before the next one is put on. All stamping and lettering to be done in aluminum leaf. Engine to be numbered on side of dome and panel of cab. Tender to be numbered on back end and lettered "N.Y.C. & H.R.R.R." on side of tank. . . .

The judges' report at the Columbian Exposition on this outstanding locomotive is of interest:

This exhibit having been assigned to me for re-examination of the Departmental Committee, I report: that it is a locomotive of great size and power, of elegant construction, built especially for high speed by one of the foremost designers of the United States; a locomotive which has attained the highest speed known to have been reached by any in the world, and while drawing its regular train. I recommend an award for excellence of design and of construction, and for superiority of performance.

A. VON BORRIES
CHARLES PAINE

Contemporary with and following the locomotive builders' pictorial advertising were those of the railroads, of express companies, and of the railroad-supply industry. Some of the examples shown on pages 93–99 include work by Currier & Ives and similar well-known printmakers. The "Railroad Scene" of Currier & Ives, it is interesting to note, was issued as almost identical advertising for the Erie Railroad, with the unmarked station of the former lettered "Hornellsville" and the locomotives carrying Erie inscriptions (page 97).

Posters, as distinguished from prints, carry much more printing, but when combined with illustrations of old engines are nearly as colorful and interesting. The greater proportion to be found are black and white, but many in two or more colors were printed, some being shown in the color section. Earlier printed matter, when cuts were employed, sometimes shows primitive locomotives and cars; but these should not be taken to indicate the kind of equipment used on the line advertised, as the cuts were more or less "standard," and available to any printer.

In recent years a large number of the old colored prints have been reproduced, particularly for calendar use. Many of these are now being collected by railroad fans.

1854

The name Norris was famous among early locomotive builders. This is one of Richard Norris's advertisements of 1854. The engine illustrated above is the "Auburn," built for the Philadelphia & Reading Railroad. In the winter of 1863–1864, the government closed down the Norris shop for refusing to do work in connection with the Civil War, and Richard's two brothers, Edward and James, went to Lancaster, Pennsylvania, leased and later bought the former Brandt Locomotive Works, continuing to build engines there for a number of years.

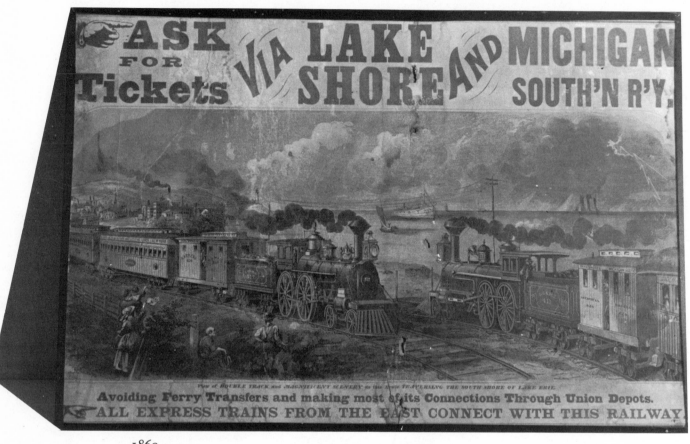

1860

"View of Double Track and Magnificent Scenery on This Route Traversing the South Shore of Lake Erie" reads part of this unusual lithograph advertising the Lake Shore & Michigan Southern Railway.

1864

The Lake Shore & Michigan Southern advertising in the 1860s was prolific. Most such posters had standard cuts of engines and cars, but "L.S.&M.S." can be read on both in this illustration. "Supper" cars are mentioned (very early dining cars), as well as "Buffalo time," before standard time was established. Another interesting note is that "The 10-25 P.M. train from Buffalo, Saturdays, will remain over Sunday at Cleveland. . . ."

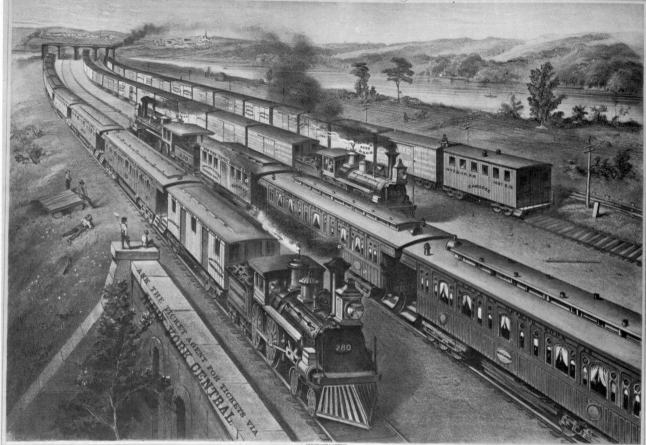

1870s

This Clay Cosack lithograph for the New York Central has a few points of interest other than advertising a 4-track railroad. The engine in the foreground has "Vanderbilt" on its tender; the "Wagner's Drawing Room Car" is "Mayflower"; most of the freight cars are Red Line or Blue Line; and an early caboose without cupola is shown.

1874

Currier & Ives made many railroad lithographs such as this one advertising the Erie Railway. This is one of their best, however inaccurate the excess lettering on locomotives and cars. These were the days when the Erie had a 6-foot gauge, which the picture seems to illustrate. The "stub" type of switch should be noted, as well as the improbable 2-6-0 type of engine at the left in passenger service.

1876

The then new suspension bridge near Niagara Falls with a typical train of the times. The lettering on the tender is "G.W.R.," and the baggage car is inscribed "Great Central Route Through Baggage Car" and "New York & Boston to Chicago & San Francisco."   *Old Print Shop, New York*

1888

Locomotive advertising of the 1880s is typically illustrated by this Manchester Locomotive Works notice of 1888. Note that Amoskeag is now part of the Manchester Works.

1892

The artist who created this fine advertising poster in 1892 was more accurate than most in his rendering of a locomotive and train. The engine is a Plant System (Atlantic Coast Line) 10-wheeler No. 11, although, of course, no tender was ever lettered for an express company, and the cars are Savannah, Florida & Western. Each box on the platform is consigned to a city such as New York, Baltimore, Wilmington, Chattanooga, or Kansas City. *Old Print Shop, New York*

chapter VI

The Locomotive as a Toy—Trackless

IT IS PROBABLE THAT THE FIRST miniatures of locomotives were actually more in the form of scale models than in that of toys. The few very early toy trains that exist seldom antedate the 1860s, when wood and tin were used to make playthings of this type. Wooden locomotives and cars had lithographed paper coverings, some remarkably well detailed, the earlier types being printed in black and white, while those coming a bit later, and which were a little more expensive, were in full colors. This method of printing the detail, rather than actually using parts, allowed economies in production, with resultant low prices. From engines only a few inches long to two feet and more, these early trains provided fair realism as well. Most locomotives had an engineer and fireman in the cab, and cars showed passengers in every window—all usually children. The more elaborate engines even had lithographed paper applied to the driving wheels, showing spokes and other details.

Some tin trains had partial paper coverings, like the wooden ones, but most were painted, and the decorative trim and names were stenciled on. The names are interesting in themselves; some were of patriotic figures, of historical prominence; others were drawn from mythology, the animal kingdom, or other sources. Among them were: "Union," "America," "U. S. Grant," "Washington," "Columbia," "Neptune," "Hercules," "Ajax," "Nero," "Giant," "Whistler," "Vulcan," "Lightning," "Jumbo," Jupiter," "Challenge," "Flash," "Rocket," "Alert," "Atlas," "Star," "Tiger," and many more.

The tin trains produced from the 1869s into the 1890s seldom had more than four wheels, generally of the 2-2-0 type. Four-wheeled tenders were usual, and a large variety of sizes, types, and trim were marketed. There were both freight and passenger trains. Of all the railroad toys made, tin trains were the most unrealistic. Perhaps that is one reason they are of considerable interest, the others being their age and ornamentation.

About 1880, the cast-iron period in toy trains began, and for about twenty years, until track trains began to replace them, iron engines and cars were made in prodigious quantities. They were durable, outlasting tin or wooden toys; better, they were more realistic. Some of the larger locomotives, even by today's standards, are close to scale models of the prototypes of the period. Not only were they better trains; they were also quite cheap, bringing wide distribution of the pull toys. Even when track trains took first place in interest, cast-iron toys were made well into the 1920s.

Like the earlier wooden and tin trains, the larger pieces were especially fine —tributes to the skill of the patternmakers and molders of the times, who of course were also making many other types of iron toys, such as fire engines, wagons, circus equipment, and bell ringers. From engines 16½ inches long without tenders, and passenger cars over 20 inches in length, down to pieces only a few inches overall, a very wide range of equipment might be chosen. The variety of locomotive types included 0-4-0, 4-2-0, 2-4-0, 4-4-0, 4-4-2, 2-6,0, 4-6-0, and even "camelbacks" and electrics, and there were a number of types of street-cars. Besides painted trains, engines and cars with nickel and bronze finishes could be had, and some of the bigger trains even had ornate stenciled trim. The patriotic theme was often evident, sets of passenger cars sometimes appearing in red, white, and blue.

HERE COME THE CARS!

By Cy. Warman.

How often at night, when I'm rocked o'er the rail,
    And the little stars shine overhead,
My mind wanders back, over memory's trail,
    And I think of the days that are dead.
The red locomotives we had for our toys,
    The coaches so gaudy and gay:
How we played together, Bill, when we were boys,
    And again I can hear you say:

"Chuchu!! Chuchu!! here comes the railroad!
    I'll be the brakeman and open the bars."
Big bell a-ringing,
    Somebody singing:
        "Chuchu!! Chuchu!! here come the cars!"

Probably the principal difficulty in collecting iron pull toys lies in identification of the manufacturer, even though this is secondary to the actual acquisition. Practically none have the maker's name, and only by learning from more experienced collectors, or by reading old catalogues can certain characteristics of a few companies be identified. Even then many are not positive, for some firms copied others, or patterns changed hands. Frequently, only a guess as to the maker of a piece is possible.

AMERICAN MANUFACTURES OF TRAINS IN WOOD, TIN, AND IRON*

ALTHOF, BERMAN & CO.	*New York*	TIN
R. BLISS MANUFACTURING CO.	*Pawtucket, R.I.*	WOOD
MILTON BRADLEY CO.	*Springfield, Mass.*	WOOD
GEORGE R. BROWN & CO.	*Forestville, Conn.*	WOOD, TIN
CARPENTER	*Port Chester, N.Y.*	IRON
CARROLLTON NOVELTY CO.	*Carrollton, Md.*	IRON
MORTON CONVERSE	*Boston, Mass.*	TIN
DENT BROTHERS	*Fullerton, Pa.*	IRON
JANES FALLOWS CO. (IXL)	*Philadelphia*	TIN
FRANCIS, FIELD & FRANCIS	*Philadelphia*	TIN
GREY IRON CASTING CO.	*Mount Joy, Pa.*	IRON
HUBLEY MANUFACTURING CO.	*Lancaster, Pa.*	IRON
HULL & STAFFORD	*Clinton, Conn.*	TIN
IVES MANUFACTURING CO.	*Bridgeport, Conn.*	TIN, IRON
KENTON HARDWARE CO.	*Kenton, Ohio*	IRON
LEO SCHLESINGER & CO.	*New York*	TIN
MERRIAM MANUFACTURING CO.	*Durham, Conn.*	TIN
PARKER BROTHERS	*Salem, Mass.*	WOOD
PRATT & LETCHWORTH ("BUFFALO")	*Buffalo, N.Y.*	IRON
W. S. REED	*Leominster, Mass.*	WOOD
WM. SHINER, SON & CO.	*Freemansburg, Pa.*	IRON
J. E. STEVENS CO.	*Cromwell, Conn.*	IRON
WILKINS TOY CO.	*Keene, N.H.*	IRON

* These do not include toy jobbers. From a table compiled by Louis Hertz.

1860s

An early tin train of the 1860s professionally restored. The background drawing accentuates the primitive appearance of such toy trains.

1870s

A wooden locomotive and train, probably by Milton Bradley. The baggage car and passenger car have some two dozen blocks each named for a fish as part of a game incorporated into the train.

1880s

Pratt & Letchworth, of Buffalo, New York, are known among collectors for making the largest well-detailed cast-iron trains. This is their version of the "999" locomotive and tender, with a combine car and a Wagner car named "Vanderbilt" (see lithograph on page 96).

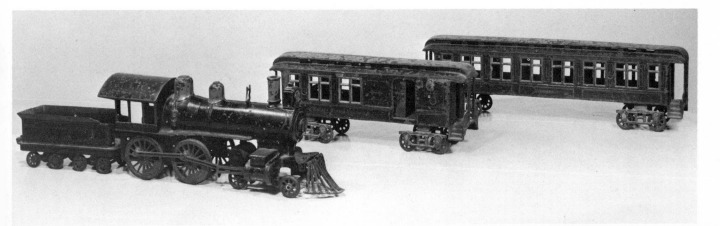

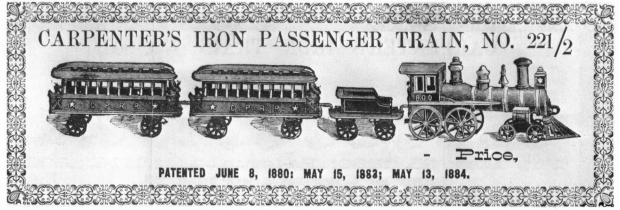

1880s

An illustration from a Carpenter catalogue of an iron floor or pull train, the latest patent date being 1884.

1900s

Ives' largest cast-iron train was this fine 4-4-0, tender and coach. The engine was handsomely painted and striped, and the passenger car was finished in bright yellow.

1900s

The smaller version of the Wilkins locomotive is this 14-inch 4-4-0 type.

1900s

A cast-iron locomotive and tender (reversed!) and a stamped sheet-metal passenger car of the early 1900s.

F. A. O. Schwarz

1901

A clockwork trackless tin locomotive made in Germany and shown in Montgomery Ward's 1901 catalogue as selling without tender for $1.98. The finish is red with black trim and brass fittings.

1912

This is an Ives cast-iron engine in the so-called "coppered" finish; with tender, it is 17 inches long. The 15½-inch passenger cars of its train have trucks of the 6-wheel type.

chapter VII

The Locomotive as a Toy—Clockwork

EXACTLY WHEN THE FIRST toy clockwork locomotive was made has not been established. Such self-propelled engines are also variously known as mechanical, spring-wound, wind-up, or key-wound. An early English clockwork-operated train, although the engine is not self-propelled, is that in the author's collection (color section). Judging by the design of the engine—the famous "single-wheeler" type—the cars, and its wooden box and printed directions, it should date from the 1840's. The mechanism is contained in a heavy lead base to which a stiff wire is attached, with the locomotive, tender and cars in turn hooked to this, whereupon the train travels in a circle around the base. This toy train is, overall, about the same scale as the present HO equipment, and is cast in lead, nicely painted and finished.

It follows logically that there must have been similar or other self-propelled engines made contemporary with this or shortly thereafter. In America, the earliest found so far are those made by George W. Brown & Co., of Hartford, Connecticut, in the late 1850s and early 1860s. Like the English train and pull-toy trains, it had no tracks, but one small swiveling wheel allowed it to be set to run straight or in circles of any radius. Though it bore only the remotest resemblance to any actual locomotive, the novelty of its being self-propelled must have created a good market. Certainly, despite their age, a number have turned up among collectors, which would seem to bear out the theory that a reasonably large quantity was produced.

Through the 1850s and into the 1890s, many and varied tin clockwork locomotives were made, Ives being perhaps the principal manufacturer. Some were quite large and handsomely finished and decorated, like the pull-toy engines of the period. When the period of the iron train followed, clockwork was used in some of them, but only in a small proportion, considering the large quantities of iron toys made. An interesting and unusual clockwork train was the circular elevated track production of Hubley's in the 1880s. Reminiscent of the mechanical English one first described, it had two clockwork motors mounted in the center to which an arm was attached, and, in turn, the engine was attached to this. Except for the stamped circular rails, all components were cast iron—engine, tender, arches, and supporting columns. Like the steam trains of Beggs, its wheels were set to run only in a circle.

The earliest track trains to have clockwork-driven locomotives were first made in Europe in the late 1880s, and in the United States immediately after the turn of the century. Most German locomotives had sheet-metal (tinplate) bodies, and are easily identifiable by the buffers instead of a pilot, or "cowcatcher." Some for export still had buffers and perhaps a bell (never used on European engines), while others had pilots; some even had both. The mechanisms were quite good; even today most of those that collectors find still function.

American-made engines generally had cast-iron bodies or superstructures (boiler and cab), whether the gauge was 0 or 1; but as they were unmarked, it is sometimes difficult to identify the early makes; most, however, were Ives. Nevertheless, a collector soon learns the characteristics of the various German trains; and unmarked Marklin, Bing, Karl Bub (KBN), Carette, and so on, can be fairly easily identified by couplers, wheels, finish, and general construction. Most of the early clockwork locomotives were either 2-2-0 or 0-4-0 types; but after a few years many 4-4-0 engines were made, a notable example being the Ives No. 40 in 1 gauge. Probably the biggest clockwork production steam type was the "Baltic" 4-6-4 of Marklin. The larger clockwork mechanisms had both forward and reverse speeds, sometimes two forward, and track trips so that engines could be stopped without touching them.

In England, especially, in the 1920s and early 1930s clockwork trains found considerable favor, model railroads being sometimes run on a timetable schedule with this type of "power." Many of the cheaper but good models were produced in Germany for English distributors. Clockwork locomotives never found much favor with model railroaders in the United States, however, although innumerable toy engines were made and sold. With the increasing interest in electric trains, their production gradually diminished, and today only a few very cheap toys of this type are still being made.

Although the subject covers steam and electric to a greater extent than it does clockwork locomotives, it might be well to mention catalogues here. These are invaluable as references—in fact a "must" for the train collector. Even before seriously collecting, a general idea of what was made and when, and by whom, is basic unless a hit-or-miss principle of acquisition is followed. Take any five or six years of Lionel catalogues, for instance, and explore the varieties of production. It will be quickly seen that, allowing for some duplication of equipment, the possibilities, considering well over sixty years of manufacturing, are surprising to a new collector. Add to this the yearly productions of Ives, American Flyer, and other American, as well as European, companies, and it will be seen that catalogues are the guidebooks to the train collectors' hobby.

Besides the original catalogues, a number of reprints of Lionel and Ives have now been published at an average price of $2.50. The Train Collectors' Association has also issued four fairly complete compilations of Lionel 0- and standard-gauge locomotives and cars in numerical order. Coupled with the association's quarterly bulletin, valuable basic information is thus continually being added to literature available on the hobby of train collecting.

1860s

An early Ives tin train with a clockwork mechanism.   *F. A. O. Schwarz*

1890s

An early Marklin clockwork 0-4-0 engine of the late 1890s. Some locomotives such as this could reverse, and track trips were provided for this contingency or for stopping. The rare side observation car is also of interest.

1890s

Some of Marklin's very early productions, from a catalogue of the 1890s, are illustrated on this page. The type of locomotive shown on page 108 can be seen at upper-right center. The track layout is worthy of note. A few of their other toys are also incorporated, although comparison of sizes is impossible. The roundhouse at lower right, for instance, is actually more than twice as large as the station.

1890s

This is part of a large Marklin 2-gauge layout with a variety of accessories and a clockwork train made for the American market. Some of the items illustrated on the catalogue page (page 109) may be seen here.

1900s

This is a window display of early 1-gauge trains set up by the Du Pont Company in Wilmington about 1960. The trains and accessories were from the author's collection.

OLD-TIME TRAINS ARE FUN TO VIEW...

TOMORROW'S TRAINS ARE BUILT FOR YOU

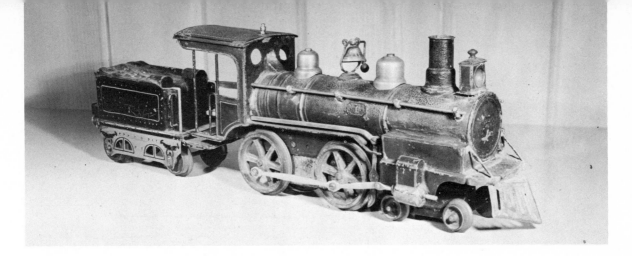

1905

Marklin made this 2-gauge clockwork engine in the early 1900s.

1907

A Bing 1-gauge American type 4-4-0 clockwork locomotive.

1910

An early American-made clockwork train of 1910. This is O gauge made by American Flyer.

Uhrwerk-Lokomotiven. Spur 0, I, II.

Mit regulierten Kraftwerken von ausgezeichneter Leistung.
Neueste, erstklassige Maschinen von schön proportionierten Formen und feinster Handlackierung.
Mit Hilfe des Uebersetzungsaufzugs und mittelst Kurbelschlüssels werden die Uhrwerke der stärksten Lokomotiven mit leichter Müh aufgezogen, so dass das Aufziehen auch für jüngere Kinder möglich ist.

FE-Typ
extra schwere
Express-Maschine
mit Doppelwer..
2 4 gekuppelt.

FE 1021 mit Tender. Mk. 60.— p. St.   FE 1022 mit Tender. Mk 62. p. St.

Lokomotive, mit Doppelwerk, vierachsig, mit Drehgestell, Tender vierachsig.
Vor- und rückwärts-, langsam- und schnellfahrend. **Mit Bremse.** Das Uhrwerk besitzt 2 Zugfedern je mit besonderem Aufzug und ist von ausserordentlicher Kraftleistung. Maschine von elegantester Konstruktion. Mit 3 Nickellaternen 2310.

Spur I 48 mm.	No. FE 1021.		Höhe . . 16,5 cm. Länge . . 37,5 cm
	Mit Tender		Länge . . 61,5 „
Spur II 54 mm.	No. FE 1022.		Höhe . . 16,5 cm. Länge . . 38 „
	Mit Tender		Länge . . 64 „

PLM-Typ
Internationale
Schnellzugs-Maschine.
2 4 gekuppelt.

E 1020 PLM. Mk. 16.70 p. St.   E 1021 PLM. Mk. 27.50 p. St.
Tender E 1801 0. „ 1.70 „   Tender E 1801 I. 3.30 „

Lokomotiven, mit reguliertem Uhrwerk, vierachsig, mit Drehgestell, Tender dreiachsig.
Umsteuerung für Vor- und Rückwärtsfahrt. **Bremse** von Hand und automatisch zu betätigen. Original-Modell, mit Luftschneideflächen. **Fahrtregulierung** für Spur I auf langsam und schnell.
Metallteile: Galeriestange, Kolbenstange, Kreuzkopfführung etc. fein vernickelt.

Spur 0 = 35 mm.	No. E 1020 PLM.		Höhe . 10,5 cm, Länge . 23,5 cm
Mit 3 Laternen 2307. Mit Tender			. . . Länge . 35,5 „
Spur I = 48 mm.	No. E 1021 PLM.		Höhe . 14,5 cm, Länge . 34,5 „
Mit automatischer Fahrtumsteuerung. Mit 2 Laternen 2308, 1 Stück 02309.			
Mit Tender			Länge . 50 „

H-Typ
Staats-Bahn
Express-
Lokomotive.
Wuchtiges,
imponierendes
Modell.
3 6 gekuppelt.

H 1021 mit Tender Mk. 55. p. St.   H 1021 1611. Mk. 60.— p. St.

H 1021 Lokomotive, mit reguliertem Kraftwerk, sechsachsig, mit 2 Drehgestellen, Tender vierachsig.
Aussergewöhnliche Dimensionen, nur verwendbar für Schienen von 180 cm Kreisdurchmesser.
Hervorragend feine Maschine von bedeutender Leistung. Reiche Metall-Garnirung, fein vernickelt.
Umsteuerung für Vor- und Rückwärtsfahrt. **Mit Bremse.**
Fahrtregulierung für langsam und schnell. 8 Laternen 02309.

H 1021 1611 Lokomotive wie zuvor, mit 16 Schienen 1611 A.

Höhe . . . . 14,5 cm	Länge . . . . 42,5 cm.
Mit Tender	Länge . . . 66,5 „

1910

A page from a Marklin catalogue, about 1910, listing some of the larger clockwork locomotives.

112

Moderne 4achsige Schnellzugslokomotive mit 4achsigem Tender.
Nach Original-Modellen des Großbetriebes gebaut.
In vollendeter Ausführung und feinster Lackierung. Mit sehr solidem, **extra starkem Uhrwerk,**
Bremsvorrichtung und Vorrichtung zum Vor- und Rückwärtsfahren.

No. 965/35	35 mm Spurweite, 44 cm lang (inkl. Tender)	. . . .	komplett Stück M. 33.—
— 965/48	48 —	— 57 — — — — —	— — — — 41.25
— 965/54	54 —	— 65 — — — — —	— — 51.—

1910

An illustration and description of a well-detailed locomotive, which is almost a scale model, from a Georges Carette catalogue of 1910. This was made in three sizes—0, 1, and 2 gauges. Below is the 1-gauge engine, the only difference being that it has a pilot instead of a buffer beam.

1915

A Karl Bub (KBN) 1-gauge clockwork locomotive and tender of about 1915. Adding a pilot to any of the German-made stock or production engines was frequently all that was necessary for export to the American trade.

chapter VIII

The Locomotive as a Toy—Steam

TOY STEAM LOCOMOTIVES MAY generally be said to date from the 1870s, although undoubtedly various individual models were built prior to that. In Europe firms such as Stevens Model Dockyard, dating back to 1843, began to make trains about 1881. The first American steam-driven toy engines were those of Eugene Beggs, their manufacture commencing in the 1870s and continuing into the early 1900s. A previously unknown manufacturer until recently was Howard & Co., one of whose locomotives is shown on page 116. Weeden was another early maker who started building such toys about 1882. All three firms used oscillating cylinders on their engines; and, based on quality, Howard was superior to Beggs, with Weeden making the cheapest train—about $2.50 for an entire set.

From the 1880s on, German locomotives came in a variety of sizes and types, Marklin and Carette making the most detailed—some rating almost "scale model" perfection. Other German firms, such as Bing and Planck, produced steam-driven engines in small gauges, those of the latter being least known and hardest for the collector to find.

All tinplate steam engines were alcohol fired, some elaborate ones even having a water pump for adding water to the boiler while under steam. These larger ones, too, had pressure gauges, water glasses, drain cocks, and safety valves. The cheaper oscillating-cylinder engines often came without safety valves, the spring-mounted cylinders serving such a purpose.

As with the imported clockwork productions, these German locomotives usually had European prototypes, and were frequently "Americanized" by additions of pilot and bell, and perhaps by lettering for such railroads as New York Central or Pennsylvania. Many were also made for the British trade, although these required more specialized design.

Except for a few adaptations of Lionel 0-gauge locomotives into electrically heated, steam-driven types by Steam Electric Co. in the early 1930s, no toy steam engines were made in the United States after the Weeden "Dart." Only a few of the Beggs productions approached in size some of the better German-made toys. In the United States these importations were sold particularly by the several Schwarz toy stores and a few of the larger department stores. Many were sold in England, and "factory specials" were often made for stores such as Gamage's and Bond's of London. Bassett-Lowke distributed numbers of them, their catalogue listings sometimes mentioning the maker's name but more often not, the simpler and smaller locomotives being merely their "cheaper" line.

Largest quantities of German production were the 2-2-0 and 0-4-0 types in 0 and 1 gauges, these frequently coming in "tank" loco form without a tender. Marklin's American 4-4-0 (page 119) in 1 gauge and their 4-6-2 in 0 and 1 (Paris-Lyon-Méditerranée, English, and German prototypes) are outstanding. Carette's American compound 4-4-0 and British "single-wheelers" in these gauges are comparable and much to be desired, but quite scarce. But *anything* in steam-driven toy locomotives is of interest to the collector, regardless of origin or prototype.

Bassett-Lowke in the early 1930s brought out a line of tinplate live steamers in 0 and 1 gauges. These were three slightly different Moguls, or 2-6-0s, on a standard chassis and with simplified outside valve gear. They were plain but good, and operated well; even today the 0-gauge version is still made, and may also be obtained in kit form.

1870s

Though the Beggs steam locomotives were first patented in the 1870s, they were made into the 1900s. They were 1 gauge, and most had their wheels preset to traverse a circle of track.

1876

One of the rarest American-made toy steam locomotives is this Howard oscillating cylinder engine of 1876. It has a brass boiler, turned brass smokestack and domes, and the gauge is 2⅛ inches, although it probably was not run on track. The Howard name, patent date, and so on, are stamped on the boiler.

1880s

This is the Weeden "Dart," the least expensive of American-made steam toy engines. It cost about $2.50.

1900s

This Marklin 0-4-0 steam locomotive was practically all brass except for its tender. Consideration for the small fry who might be operating it is evidenced by the wooden coverings on the handrails—to avoid burned fingers. This is 1 gauge.

1900s

Largest of all toy steam locomotives (as opposed to scale) is this extremely rare Marklin 4-4-0. Approximately on a scale of 1 inch to the foot, and with a 4⅝-inch gauge, it is 4 feet 4 inches in length. In a sense it is actually an enlarged version of the 1- or 2-gauge engines.

1910

Bing made this British-type 2-gauge 4-4-0 tank engine in 1910. The "Pilot" was steam driven and, like all others, alcohol fired.

Krames Collection

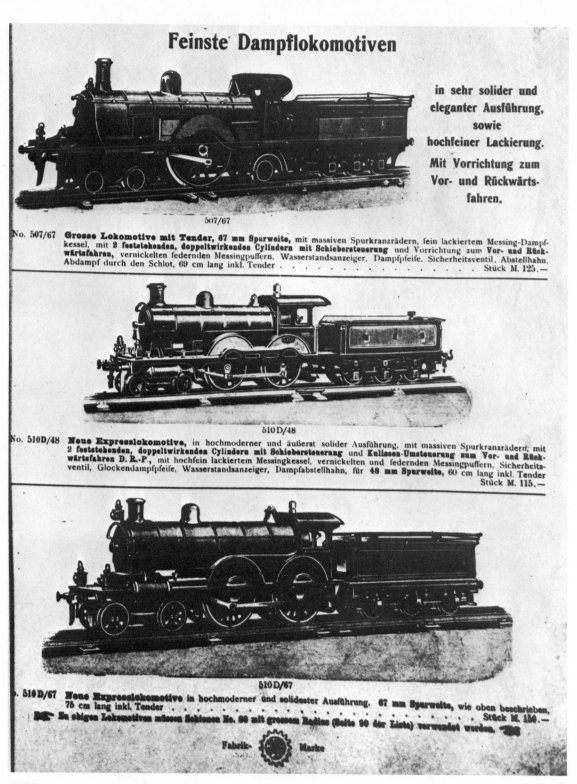

Feinste Dampflokomotiven

in sehr solider und eleganter Ausführung, sowie hochfeiner Lackierung.

Mit Vorrichtung zum Vor- und Rückwärtsfahren.

507/67

No. 507/67 **Grosse Lokomotive mit Tender, 67 mm Spurweite**, mit massiven Spurkranzrädern, fein lackiertem Messing-Dampfkessel, mit 2 feststehenden, doppeltwirkenden Cylindern mit Schiebersteuerung und Vorrichtung zum **Vor- und Rückwärtsfahren**, vernickelten federnden Messingpuffern, Wasserstandsanzeiger, Dampfpfeife, Sicherheitsventil, Abstellhahn, Abdampf durch den Schlot, 69 cm lang inkl. Tender . . . . Stück M. 125.—

510 D/48

No. 510D/48 **Neue Expresslokomotive**, in hochmoderner und äußerst solider Ausführung, mit massiven Spurkranzrädern, mit 2 feststehenden, doppeltwirkenden Cylindern mit Schiebersteuerung und **Kulissen-Umsteuerung zum Vor- und Rückwärtsfahren D. R.-P.**, mit hochfein lackiertem Messingkessel, vernickelten und federnden Messingpuffern, Sicherheitsventil, Glockendampfpfeife, Wasserstandsanzeiger, Dampfabstellhahn, für **48 mm Spurweite**, 60 cm lang inkl. Tender Stück M. 115.—

510 D/67

No. 510D/67 **Neue Expresslokomotive** in hochmoderner und solidester Ausführung. 67 mm Spurweite, wie oben beschrieben, 75 cm lang inkl. Tender . . . . Stück M. 150.—
☞ Zu obigen Lokomotiven müssen Schienen No. 90 mit grossem Radius (Seite 90 der Liste) verwendet werden. ☜

Fabrik-   Marke

1910

A page from a Carette catalogue illustrating steam locomotives that are almost classifiable as models rather than as toys. These are from British prototypes, and were intended for that market.

118

1910

Catering to the American market, Marklin made this 1-gauge 4-4-0 steamer about 1910. It is somewhat more detailed than many of their engines and has track-tripped reversing gear.

1912

At the left is a Bing o-gauge oscillating-cylinder reversible steam locomotive. Another, simpler, o-gauge 0-4-0 is the Marklin engine at the right.

1920s

Marklin made the Paris-Lyons-Mediterranean Pacific in steam, clockwork, and electric propulsion for a number of years. This is a 1-gauge steamer "factory restored" by Marklin.

1920s

A typical Marklin steam 0-4-0 is represented by this 1-gauge engine.

No. 297   **THE "ROYAL MAIL."**

A Locomotve Engine on 6 wheels, Polished Bright Brass Boiler, 8½ in. long, 2½ in. diameter, with Longitudinal stay bolt from end to end, 2 cast Rings shrunk on round the boiler, making the boiler very strong and safe, Steam Dome, Bell, Whistle, Ramsbottom Safety Valve, 2 Gauge Taps, Regulator, Signal Lamp, Buffers, Line Clearers, Hand Rails, Coupling Chain, Cab, Splashers, 2 Eccentrics with automatic reversing motion, Steam Pipes, Connecting Rods, 2 correct pattern Slide Valve Cylinders, ¾ in. bore, 1¼ in. stroke, will run backwards or forwards, circular or straight, on a floor or rails, or parts screwed together, total length 15½ in., painted and lined in colours. *Our own make from brass and steel castings.* Price £6 7s. 6d. This Engine fitted with Bogie Carriage and eight Wheels, 14/- extra.

Circular Rail 25 ft. in circumference, mounted on strong wood base, price £2 10s. 0d. (see page 52). Polished Mahogany wood **Carriages** and **Guard's Vans** 30/- each. Trucks 18/6 and 21/6 each. Brake Vans 22/6 each (see page 51).

No. 298   **THE "CONQUEROR."**

Locomotive Engine on 8 wheels with Bogie Truck in front, Bright Polished Brass Boilers 8½ in. long, 2½ in. diameter, with Longitudinal stay bolt from end to end, 2 cast Rings shrunk on round the boiler, making the boiler very strong and safe, Steam Dome, Ramsbottom Safety Valve, Bell, Whistle, 2 Gauge Taps, Regulator, Signal Lamp, Buffers, Line Clearers, Hand Rails, Coupling Chain, Cab, Splashers, 2 Eccentrics with automatic reversing motion, Steam Pipes, Connecting Rods, 2 correct pattern Slide Valve Cylinders ¾ in, bore, 1½ in. stroke, will run backwards or forwards, circular or straight, on a floor or rails, all parts screwed together, total length 16 in., painted and lined in colours. *Our own make from brass and steel castings.* Price £7 10s. 0d.

Circular Rails, Carriages, Trucks, &c., are the same size and prices as for "Royal Mail" Locomotives.

1924

The Stevens Model Dockyard in London was one of the earliest of all toy and model firms, and continued in business until bombed out in World War II. From the 1880s on, they supplied a variety of miniature locomotives. Although this page is from a 1924 catalogue, the cuts are identical to those dating back thirty or more years. A "Royal Mail" engine identical with this illustration may be seen in the color section. The gauge is 2⅞ inches.

120

Dampflokomotiven
Locomotives à vapeur
Locomotoras a vapor

Spurweite — Voie — Ancho de la vía 0 = 35 mm

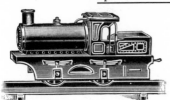

11/22/0

Lokomotive 17 cm lang, geschliffener Messingkessel, **oscillie-render** Dampfzylinder

Locomotive, longueur 17 cm, chaudière en cuivre poli mat, cylindre **oscillant**

Locomotora 17 cm de largo, ealdera de latón pulido mate y cilindro **oscilante**

11/21/0

Lokomotive 19 cm lang, blau patinierter Messingkessel, **2 os-cillierende** vernickelte Dampfzylinder, Dampfpfeife, Tender 11 cm lang

Locomotive, longueur 19 cm, chaudière en cuivre patiné bleu, 2 cylindres **oscillants** nickelés, sifflet à vapeur, tender 11 cm

Locomotora 19 cm de largo, caldera de latón patinado azul, 2 cilindros **oscilantes** niquelados, silbato a vapor, ténder 11 cm

11/23/0

Lokomotive 17 cm lang, matt geschliffener Messingkessel, **oscillierender** Dampfzylinder, Tender 8,5 cm lang

Locomotive, longueur 17 cm, chaudière en cuivre poli mat, cylindre **oscillant,** tender 8,5 cm

Locomotora 17 cm de largo, caldera de latón pulido **mate** y cilindro **oscilante,** ténder 8,5 cm

11/24/0

Lokomotive 22 cm lang, blau patinierter Messingkessel, Glockendampfpfeife, **2 feststehende** Dampfzylinder, **Vor-und Rückwärtsfahrt durch Handumsteuerung,** Tender 14 cm lang

Locomotive, longueur 22 cm, chaudière en cuivre patiné bleu, 2 cylindres **fixes,** sifflet à vapeur forme cloche, **marche avant et arrière, changement de marche à la main,** ténder 14 cm

Locomotora 22 cm de largo, caldera de latón patinado **azul,** 2 cilindros **fijos, marcha hacia adelante y atrás, cambio manual de marcha,** silbato a vapor forma campana, ténder 14 cm

Spurweite — Voie — Ancho de la vía I = 48 mm

11/21/1

Lokomotive 22 cm lang, blau patinierter Messingkessel, Dampfpfeife, **2 oscillierende** vernickelte Dampfzylinder, Tender 13 cm lang

Locomotive, longueur 22 cm, chaudière en cuivre patiné bleu, 2 cylindres **oscillants** nickelés, sifflet à vapeur, tender 13 cm

Locomotora 22 cm de largo, caldera de latón patinado azul, 2 cilindros **oscilantes** niquelados, silbato a vapor, ténder 13 cm

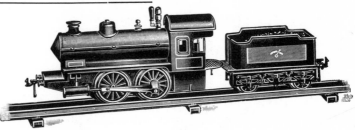

11/24/1

Lokomotive 26 cm lang, blau patinierter Messingkessel, Glockendampfpfeife, **2 feststehende** Dampfzylinder, **Vor-und Rückwärtsfahrt durch Handumsteuerung,** Tender 16 cm lang

Locomotive, longueur 26 cm, chaudière en cuivre patiné bleu, 2 cylindres **fixes,** sifflet à vapeur forme cloche, **marche avant et arrière, changement de marche à la main,** tender 16 cm

Locomotora 26 cm de largo, caldera de latón patinado azul, 2 cilindros **fijos, marcha hacia adelante y atrás, cambio manual de marcha,** silbato a vapor forma campana, ténder 16 cm

chapter IX

The Locomotive as a Toy—Electric

EVERY COLLECTOR OF TOY TRAINS has, of course, his personal preferences. Some want only iron pull trains, others only a particular gauge; still others collect only certain makes, while others limit their interests to a period of manufacturing or a certain type of propulsion. This sort of specializing is largely brought about by space limitations as a collection grows or as an enthusiast discovers certain features or equipment that appeals to him.

"Electric Trains" as a general heading would exclude the pull toys, clockwork or steam-propelled locomotives, as well as certain makers, but encompass all the rest. Most collectors probably favor this group. From the middle 1890s on, these have been what most boys desired, and mention of the names of some of the first American manufacturers in the field, such as Carlisle & Finch, Howard, Elektoy, and Voltamp make any collector sit up and take notice. Next came the more familiar names—Lionel, Ives, American Flyer, Boucher, and Dorfan. Though most catalogues were addressed to boys, Boucher's approach was a bit different; their slogan was "Buy one for your boy for yourself."

Beginning in the 1890s, electric trains were imported from Europe, particularly the work of Marklin and Carette and, later, Bing and Karl Bub. Like their clockwork productions, the more elaborate locomotives of the first two manufacturers were practically scale models, with much more realism than American-made ones. These came in three gauges—O, 1, and standard, while Marklin, for instance, often made the identical piece in 1¼ inches, 1¾, 2, 2½, and even larger gauges.

It required the scale-model railroad hobbyists of the 1930s, with their demand for realism, to spur American manufacturers into making their trains more to scale, the peak of this trend being reached with Lionel's "700" Hudson and 6-wheel switcher.

A vital and often discussed point concerning condition of old toy trains is whether or not to restore. "Restoring" means, of course, to put the piece into a condition as close as possible to its appearance when it left the factory. There has been some opposition to restoring, but it has been based primarily upon the many pieces that some youngster or amateur has spoiled by "repairing" them with cheap paint, usually of another color. Such pieces are often restorable, but unless they are the rarer items, it seldom is worth the time or effort. They should be distinguished from genuinely restored pieces by the term "repainted."

It is not fair to state dogmatically that to restore a piece lessens its value. If it has already been repainted, or if most of its paint is gone or it is rusted, having it professionally restored will certainly increase its value. If a piece has only a few scratches, it would be folly to do it over; but if it is in very poor condition, and rare enough to be worth restoring, it would certainly seem much more desirable to have it as presentable as when new. There is also the esthetic value to be considered; surely a collection of tinplate in good condition is infinitely more attractive to contemplate than one that looks like an accumulation of junk.

The situation is analogous to that of restoring old automobiles. No one who acquires such a machine ever leaves it in the condition it is usually found in—rusted, with parts missing, and finish poor. Such cars are always restored as nearly as possible to their pristine condition. Antique furniture, old paintings, guns—almost anything old is restored if necessary, and the same may legitimately be applied to old trains. One qualification should be made, however. To avoid any confusion in future identification, the piece should somewhere be marked "Restored," preferably with the craftsman's name and date.

Almost all collectors, despite the claims of a few purists, have in some way done some restoring. The replacing of wheels or missing trim, such as bells or headlights, can technically be called "restoring," for it is not only the finish or the paint that is involved. But each collector to his own interests. How or what he collects and what he does with it are his own business entirely. This, in general, sums up the principles of the Train Collectors Association, Inc., the outstanding group of collectors pursuing this hobby.

Inevitably, the question of values is one of the most important and most often discussed topics among collectors, but there is no standard guide, such as stamp collectors may find in an accepted catalogue. Naturally, the older American-made tinplate items from before, say, 1915 command higher prices, but there are also other trains from that period that are not particularly valuable. Conversely, even into the 1930s there are certain locomotives or trains of which few were made and which are consequently worth more than some thirty years older. Large production runs of engines such as Lionel No. 33 (there are some variations worth several times the commonest type), No. 8, No. 10, and their corresponding cars, indicate that there will have to be many more collectors before a saturation point is reached and values increase over the present minimum. As with any other hobby, value is based strictly upon scarcity rather than upon age. Many a train has been discovered in an attic, with its finder, if he is not a collector, thinking he has something rare, only to be disillusioned. Some antique dealers unfamiliar with the subject quote fantastic prices—but no one *has* to pay such prices. Some novices research with catalogues; but learning from other collectors soon enables a newcomer at least to distinguish generally whether something is reasonably priced or not.

1880s

One of the earliest electrically driven steam-type locomotives is this 4-2-0. Semiproduction items, such as certain engine parts, indicate that it was not a homemade toy. The motor is Electro Dynamic and is of a type made by this company, then in Philadelphia, in 1882; possibly the entire train was their make. The engine and tender are about 25 inches in length, and the track gauge is 4 inches.

1905

An early Marklin electric locomotive of the "high voltage" type, so called because it was used on 110 volts reduced somewhat through lamp resistances to about 60 or 70 of actual operating current. This is a 1-gauge American type.

Krames Collection

1916

A Bing electric 4-4-0 in 1 gauge lettered for the Pennsylvania Railroad about 1916.

1916

An Ives advertisement from the *St. Nicholas Magazine* of 1916. The No. 1129 engine is also illustrated below.

1916

The Ives No. 1129 locomotives in their 1916 catalogue were shown as 4-4-0 types. However, this 1129 is a 2-4-2. Like most of their others, it has a cast-iron boiler or superstructure.

1920s

Very few "standard-gauge" (2⅛") locomotives were made in Germany, but here is one of the exceptions, a Marklin 4-4-0 lettered "Pennsylvania Rail Road."   *Krames Collection*

1923

The last of the nickel and brass Lionel No. 7 4-4-0 engines were made in 1923. This is one of the particularly desirable collectors' items.

1929

An Italian-made Pacific of the British "Iron Duke" in 1 gauge. The F. Biaggi Company of Milan made this electrically driven engine about 1929.

1930

Near the end of Bing's production, this Pacific type in 1 gauge was their largest electric locomotive. From their last catalogue.

1950s

A cartoon from *Esquire* showing that the train hobby is not only for the younger generation.

"Now this one has a feature you'll like. If your kid monkeys with it while you're at the office this car explodes and scares hell out of him"

1931

Samuel M. Vauclain, Chairman of the Board of the Baldwin Locomotive Works, is shown here with his three grandsons, Billy, Sam, and Henriques Hamilton, in 1931. The trains are Lionel o gauge with one of their first steam-type locomotives, apparently a No. 258.

1920

Lionel advertised in a number of magazines. This example is from a *Popular Science Monthly* of 1920.

128

1910, 1920s

Not steam, but of interest because they are the two prototypes for most of the electric toy locomotives made. Above is an engine of the New York Central; below is one of the Milwaukee Road.

There are plenty of old German pieces, for instance, some of which may be fifty years old, that are still to be had quite reasonably. Ives and Lionel equipment from the 1920s is fairly plentiful today, and not expensive, so the cost of collecting need not trouble a newcomer too much. Thus, as there are no scales of prices for tinplate, the law of supply and demand rules. At a collectors' meeting, such as a Train Collectors' Association Convention, where everyone brings duplicates to trade or sell, when price is discussed there is a favorite quip, "Am I buying or selling?"

One of the biggest thrills of collecting is in finding the proverbial "sleeper"— a good, perhaps rare, piece at a much lower than expected price, or in having such an item presented by a friend. An unexpected windfall of this sort makes up for weeks or months of turning up ordinary things. To display such a piece of tinplate to other collectors, or just to experience the joy of possession, gives its owner exactly the same kind of satisfaction enjoyed by collectors of any other sort, whether they acquire books, guns, china, glass, paintings, or anything else.

GAUGES AND SCALES USED FOR TINPLATE

GAUGE	SCALE	DESIGNATION	DESCRIPTION
12 mm	1/10", 3 mm	TT	
16.5 mm	3.5 mm	HO	Bing Clockwork 1922 Bing Electric 1924
¾", 19 mm	4 mm	OO	"HO" European designation Lionel 1938–42, Scalecraft
⅞"	3/16"	S	American Flyer 1945 to present
1", 1⅛"	—	—	German clockwork 1910–25
1¼", 32 mm	¼" or 7 mm	O	European since 1890s U.S. since 1904
1¾", 45 mm	⅜" or 10 mm	1	European since 1890s U.S. (Ives, Elektoy) 1912–22
1⅞"	—	—	Beggs, Weeden 1870s–1900s
2" or 51 mm		2	European 1890s–1920s Voltamp 1900s–1920s
2⅛"	approx. ⅜"	Standard	U.S. 1908–38
2½"	½"	3	European 1890s–1910
2⅞"	—	—	Lionel 1901–05
3¼"	9/16"	—	Buddy-L 1929–36
4"	—	—	European
4⅝"	——	—	Marklin

Note: Measurements given in old catalogues of toy trains were from centers of rails, not between as is properly gauged. Thus 0 gauge was given as 1⅜" (European, 35 mm), 1 gauge 48 mm, and "Standard" 2¼".

chapter X

The Locomotive in Miniature—Small-Scale Models

THE SMALL-SCALE MODEL locomotives described in this chapter must first be distinguished from toy or "tinplate" productions. There is undoubtedly some overlapping, it must be admitted; for manufacturers of toy trains today make their products much more realistic than they were some years ago, and many are practically scale models. But even fifty and more years ago German and English toymakers were making deluxe toy trains that were very close to scale, well detailed and excellently finished. However, scale-model locomotives are more properly thought of as individually made miniatures requiring many hours of painstaking work to build. Before the advent of HO gauge and its present domination of the hobby market, detailed O gauge, or ¼-inch-scale, locomotives were the goal of most model railroaders. The illustrations accompanying this chapter are largely of such models made through the 1930s, and indicate the possibilities of this scale, which currently appears to be making a comeback. O-gauge parts, sets of castings and drawings, and many finished models are becoming available once more. Custom models of good workmanship and quality have become much-desired collectors' items.

Some of the foregoing remarks might also apply to HO gauge, for many enthusiasts are building up collections of custom-built engines in this size. The greater proportion of those available or previously sold are imports, some having a very limited production run, which increases their desirability.

In England, where the weekly *Model Engineer* had been published since the 1890s, a new magazine, *The Model Railway News*, appeared in 1925. In Britain there had been several sizes of small-scale model railways for years, but it was not until the late 1920s that a small amount of interest in scale O gauge began to develop in the United States.

It required the Century of Progress in Chicago in 1933, with its several ¼-inch-scale layouts displayed by various railroads, to spark a national interest in the hobby. The exhibit built by the author for the Chesapeake & Ohio was the first really large O-gauge layout, some 80 feet in length, on which three trains ran continuously, two being pulled by models of what were then the largest two-cylindered engines in the world. With the publication of *Model Craftsman* (now *Railroad Model Craftsman*) the following year, and shortly thereafter the *Model Railroader*, the hobby was well launched and O gauge was the preferred size. Most club layouts used this ¼-inch scale, and a number still do, for it assures the best in performance and detail. HO began to be more and more in evidence through the late 1930s because of the smaller space required and because it was less expensive. After World War II, with the help of die castings and plastic molding, and for the same reasons of economy, HO has become the gauge most used. A few other even smaller gauges, such as TT and OOO, were introduced, and also have their adherents; but these are more for operational layouts than for modeling the iron horse. The fact remains that engines can be much more faithfully reproduced in miniature in the larger scales.

Just as among a few careless artists, and in the film industry, where insufficient or inaccurate research has resulted in erroneous pictures of the iron horse, so have some firms in the model field produced spurious locomotives or kits. Though very few alleged locomotives were so ridiculous in appearance and in the claims made for them that not even a layman would be fooled, the overworked and misleading adjective "authentic" was nevertheless used in advertising them. Of all locomotives, the "General" continues to be the one most misrepresented; for, as most railroad buffs know, the famous engine in its present rebuilt form is merely representative of any form of motive power of the 1870s or 1880s rather than a restoration of its appearance at the time of the Civil War. Fortunately, the more reputable firms today offer better and more realistic locomotive models, thanks to the increased attention being paid to research, with resulting faithfulness to prototypes.

Pertinent to the field of smaller scale models is a description of how Hollywood used them in the early days of the silent movies. The series of photographs on pages 134–138 were made by Eddie Sargeant, who was special-effects cameraman and prop man for the old Vitagraph Studios from 1919 to 1923. For years Sargeant was also associated with D. W. Griffith, creating many wonderful special effects for Griffith's films. Eddie, second from the left in the picture on page 134, poses with his Vitagraph crew behind the partly completed model locomotive to be used in the wreck scene.

The second picture is a bird's-eye view of the platform used to shoot the trick train and car wreck, the scale used being about ¾ inch to the foot. Concealed wires pulled the engine and auto to their violent contact. On impact, explosive charges of powder and dust were ignited for realism. The camera shot was from a low angle so that the small-scale hills blended into the distant ones.

The third photograph shows how the wreck looked from the motion-picture camera's point of view. The concealed pull-wires on the locomotive were unwound to the point of impact, then rewound, ready for the take. In this scene the engine is, of course, now complete with Southern Pacific Lines lettering.

In scene Four the locomotive crashes into the auto. Black engine smoke was created with a mixture of resin and gunpowder. The effect of steam was obtained with a blend of magnesium and yellow powder. Concealed tubes released dust to give added realism. To give the scene "heavy" realism, the camera was cranked at 32 frames per second rather than the usual timing of 16.

GAUGES AND SCALES USED IN MODEL RAILROADING

GAUGE	SCALE	DESIGNATION	DESCRIPTION
9 mm	2 mm	OOO	Smallest practical electrical operation
.471″	4 mm	TT	"Table Top," H. P. Products
16.5 mm	.138 or 3.5 mm	HO	Developed from tinplate HO
¾″	4 mm	OO	Nason, others 1930s
⅞″	3/16″ or 5 mm	S or H1	"CD," Cleveland 1930s
1 3/16″	¼″	Q	Infrequently used in place of O
1¼″	¼″ or 7 mm	O	Developed from tinplate O
¾″	¼″	HO3	Narrow-gauge scale
1¾″	⅜″ or 10 mm	I	From tinplate I
2″		II	From tinplate (rare)
2½″	½″	3	1/24th actual size
3½″	¾″		1/18th actual size
4¾″ or 5″	1″		1/12th actual size
7¼″ or 7½″	1½″		1/8th actual size
9″ to 10½″	2″		1/6th actual size
12″	2½″		1/5th actual size
15″, 20″, 24″ and larger			

A

Ward Kimball Collection

B

Photo by Eddie Sargeant
Ward Kimball Collection

(A) Special-effects crew. (B) The setting. (C) Approaching the climax. (D) The wreck. See also text, pages 132-133.

A

B

136

C

D

1920s

This series of pictures by Eddie Sargeant shows another type of accident staged with the use of models. The first (A) is the prototype for the model, Union Pacific 10-wheeler No. 1594, and the second (B) is of the model. (C) shows the miniature setup for the dynamite wreck that was shot on the platform illustrated in the other series. This is the camera angle to be used in the final scene. In (D) the camera catches the wreck a split second before the explosion. Breakaway pieces were incorporated in the boxcar for realistic effect. The miniature train explodes in (E). In (F) nothing is left of the boxcar except debris. (G) and (H) show angles of the wrecked engine afterward. The miniature ties were on stilts, which were tripped by small powder charges, causing the locomotive to tip over toward the camera.

E

F

G

H

1880s

A ½-inch-scale wooden model of a Pennsylvania Railroad "D" class 4-4-0 built by George Niece, Master of Machinery on the Belvidere-Delaware Railroad Division at Lambertville, New Jersey, in the 1880s. This is complete in detail, even to boiler fittings, oil and tallow pots and lanterns.

1920s

A ½-inch-scale model of the Hudson & Mohawk's De Witt Clinton locomotive and tender at the Hagley Museum, Wilmington, Delaware.

1928

The "Pocasset" and "Androscoggin," two ½-inch-scale models electrically driven for two-rail track, built in the late 1920s by Albert Kelley of Philadelphia.

1930s

This is the prizewinning Royal Blue train, best model in ¼-inch scale in the contest of the late 1930s conducted by *Railroad Model Craftsman* and won by Fletcher Speed.

1930s

Part of a 16-foot model of a bit of English countryside with an LMS and two other locomotives in o gauge.

Author's layout

1931

A scene on the author's o-gauge "Penn Eastern" layout in New Rochelle, New York, in the early 1930s. The engines shown are Pennsylvania Railroad prototypes, an M1a, K4s, L1s, with the tender of a B6sb switcher.

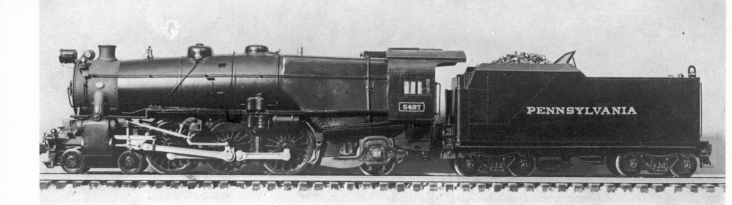

1933

A model of one of the famous K4 Class Pacifics of the Pennsylvania Railroad in ¼-inch scale.

Alexander

1934

A popular o-gauge freight locomotive, this model was also obtainable in kit form. The prototype is a Chesapeake & Ohio K3a Mikado.

Alexander

1935

This is a presentation model in ¼-inch scale of a Louisiana & Arkansas Railroad Mikado type that was presented to the Governor of Louisiana.

Alexander

1935

A ¼-inch model of a Pennsylvania Railroad Class P 4-4-0 type of engine of 1893.

Alexander

1935

This is a Pennsylvania Railroad mountain type 4-8-2 built in ¼-inch scale.

Alexander

1937

A ¼-inch scale model of a 4-4-0 locomotive of 1900. The cars, however, are of a much earlier vintage—the 1860s!

Author's layout

1938

One of the New Haven's then new Hudson engines in ¼-inch scale.

Alexander

1938

This is a ⅜-inch-scale model of the first Baldwin locomotive, the "Black Hawk," for the Philadelphia & Trenton Railroad of 1835.

Alexander

1938

The "John Bull" of the Camden & Amboy Railroad as it appeared about 1833 with pilot added. This is modeled in ⅜-inch scale.

Alexander

1939

Here is the model S-1 locomotive the Pennsylvania Railroad exhibited at the Golden Gate Exposition in San Francisco in 1939. It was also used to illustrate their various folders and brochures. The model is ¼-inch scale, and approximately 36 inches long.

Alexander

1940

A fine example of custom modeling in ¼-inch scale. This is a Boston & Albany suburban tank locomotive of the 1920s. The builder is unknown.

1940s

An o-gauge New Haven Pacific type is represented by this model. The builder is unknown.

1945

This is the famous "999" modeled in ¼-inch scale and presented to the Smithsonian Institution by the New York Central Railroad. It was exhibited with a train of the old Wagner passenger cars to represent the Empire State Express.

Alexander

1945

The modern Empire State Express for comparison with the original train was also presented to the Smithsonian Institution. This is its locomotive, a J3a Hudson type.

Alexander

1950s

A ¼-inch-scale model of the De Witt Clinton locomotive built from a detailed all-metal kit designed by the author.

1953

An excellent complete o-gauge model of a Pennsylvania Railroad I1s decapod freight locomotive ready for painting, built by George Stock.

1950s

An advertisement of the early 1950s with
an illustration of what purports to be a
"model" locomotive. This caricature of an
engine indicates the inability of some
manufacturers to research a subject
properly.

1959

A model of a typical old 4-4-0 engine of the 1870s built for the United States Information Service in 1959.
A duplicate of this was the pilot model for the American Flyer production shown below.

Alexander

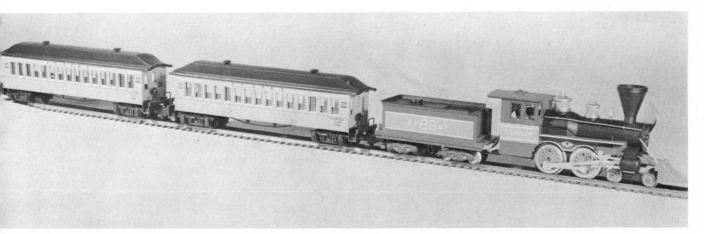

149

1961

The "Quigley," Louisville & Nashville No. 20 of the Civil War era, modeled in ½-inch scale for the National Park Service and on exhibit at Fort Donelson National Military Park. The prototype was built by Moore & Richardson in 1859.

1961

A Grant Locomotive Works 2-4-2 locomotive modeled in ¼-inch scale. The lettering on the tender is for the United States Military Railroads.

Alexander

chapter XI

The Locomotive in Miniature—Large-Scale Models

FOR ALMOST AS LONG as full-size locomotives have been manufactured, large-scale working steam models have also been built. Matthias Baldwin's first locomotive was a model that he made and installed at the Philadelphia Museum with the assistance of its manager, Franklin Peale. A track was laid in a room of this building, and upon it the little locomotive was operated, beginning on April 25, 1831. It pulled two cars carrying four persons, often twice as many, and crowds came to see for the first time in Philadelphia a practical demonstration of the use of steam for railroad motive power. Most passenger-hauling miniatures have since run outdoors.

The many fairs and expositions, such as the Centennial, the Columbian, the St. Louis, and most others, all had extensive trackage, with steam locomotives. Almost all amusement parks also had train rides, some of the locomotives being excellent miniatures, while others were more utilitarian, Cagney Brothers of Jersey City building many of the latter.

Among these larger miniature lines, that at Venice, California, is one of the more noteworthy. Built about 1905 to a scale of 4 inches to the foot, its locomotives were designed by John J. Coit and built by the Johnson Machine Works in Los Angeles. The two Prairie-type 2-6-2 engines were 19 feet 8 inches long, 4 feet 11 inches high, weighed over 11,000 pounds in working order, and had 20-inch drivers, airbrakes, MCB couplers, and acetylene headlights. About 175 pounds of steam pressure were carried, and 33 horsepower was developed. The track was 18-inch gauge, and about 2 miles long.

Among more private lines a slightly earlier one in Pennsylvania was first described in the *Locomotive Engineer* in 1890. This was a 2-inch-scale railroad at Drifton, Pennsylvania, about a mile long with 8-pound rail, two turntables, and signals. Its locomotives were designed and built by Daniel Coxe, a grandson of the locomotive builder Richard Norris, with the help of J. A. Beltz. Four engines were built, the third being a PRR 4-4-0. The engine illustrated was completed in 1895 (page 154).

All such engines were literally handmade, from the patterns to the machining and assembling, for there were no standard parts to be had, except such fittings as valves and injectors. In the middle 1890s, following the publicity accorded the record-breaking "999," sets of castings in three scales were advertised (page 155), and some engines built from them are still in existence. Later, particularly in the 1920s other large-scale locomotive castings and parts were offered hobbyists, the suppliers being H. J. Coventry of Baltimore, Frank Birch of Adrian, Michigan, and Roy Ashley of San Francisco. At present such parts in various scales may be obtained from about four sources in the United States.

Overseas the term applied to these larger-scale live-steamers and tracks was "garden railways," and Bassett-Lowke, Ltd., has supplied locomotives and components for them since the 1890s. Today several custom builders in England cater to this field, and castings and parts may be obtained from at least three firms.

Building a live-steam model locomotive is, of course, a project for a craftsman, and requires more machine tools than are ordinarily found in the average home workshop. It will take many months, perhaps a year or more of spare-time labor, albeit enjoyable, to build a real iron horse in miniature, and after it has been completed comes the pleasure of operating it. Some builders derive most of their enjoyment and relaxation in the construction of the engine, with interest subsequently waning in its operation.

There is, however, an indescribable thrill in opening the throttle of a live steamer and feeling it take hold on the rails, and then controlling it, that surpasses any other form of model railroading. There is a feeling of "aliveness" in one of these engines that proves it the close kin it is to its full-sized brother. Without question, here is the acme of railroading in miniature.

The alternative for the would-be engineer who hasn't the time or the shop ability to build one is, of course, to purchase a custom-made (they all are) live steamer and have the fun of driving it. One still has the track construction to take care of, and this is no easy matter. The roadbed must be very well built and graded, or derailments will occur, and these can be dangerous. The larger engines have been known to turn over on occasion and injure their operators, but such occurrences are rare. Still, a really good roadbed is essential for safe and satisfactory operation.

These miniature iron horses are far removed from toys; they are actually small steam locomotives that carry a high boiler pressure (100 to 150 pounds), and must be carefully controlled. From the building of the fire, getting up steam, lubricating them, keeping the proper water level, and handling the throttle correctly, they must be treated like their big relatives. To run one is great fun, but they must also be treated seriously. Their operations is quite different from throwing a switch and running a miniature electric locomotive.

Live-steamers have surprising power for their size: even a ½-inch-scale engine is capable of hauling several people. A ¾-inch-scale engine may pull a load of six to ten persons, while one in the 1½-inch scale may handle a load of fifteen to thirty people, depending upon conditions and the type of locomotive.

It must be admitted that a live steamer is somewhat expensive; much time and material go into one, whether home or custom made. There is a sort of "back door" to this kind of outdoor railroading, however, whereby one can start such a line and operate it before a live-steam locomotive is acquired, and that is to purchase or build a gas-driven locomotive, which is comparatively inexpensive. These use 1½-horsepower engines, and can be had for 7½-inch-gauge track, together with very reasonable trucks and other components. They are so safe, having a constant speed of three or four miles an hour controlled by a single clutch lever, that even a four-year-old may operate one. Even when one later puts a live steamer into service, the gas locomotive is convenient to have for standby use or for the younger generation to operate.

There are a number of historic miniature iron horses in the United States, some of which are still in use. Most are in museums or parks, and a sampling of their locations is given in the appendix, as is a listing of museums where they may also be found or where models are exhibited.

1880s

In the late 1880s four excellent examples of miniature steam locomotives were built at Drifton, Pennsylvania, by Daniel Coxe, a grandson of the famous early locomotive builder Richard Norris. Encouraged by his father, who built a complete machine shop for him, Coxe designed and built, together with an assistant, J. A. Beltz, engines that were one sixth actual size. The first was built in 1887 and the last in 1895. No. 3 was a model of a Pennsylvania Railroad class K 4-4-0, and No. 4 was more of a freelance design. The little railroad upon which they ran was a mile long, had a grade of 237 feet in the mile, had standard Lehigh Valley–type switch stands and semaphore signals, a turntable at each end, and was laid with 8-pound rail. Seven flatcars constituted the rolling stock, and with 140 pounds' steam pressure a speed of 20 miles an hour was attained.

154

1895

1898

Early advertisements of scale castings for live-steam locomotive models that appeared in *Locomotive
Engineering* during the 1890s.

January, 1898.   LOCOMOTIVE ENGINEERING.   39

1907

The locomotives of the Venice Miniature Railway were Prairie types one third actual size. The tender
lettering states weight of engine "8000 lb., tender 3127 lb., water 150 gal., oil 75 gal."

155

1907

No. 1 of the Venice Railway on the turntable. In this view there is nothing to indicate that it is other than a full-size engine.

1919

1½-inch scale model of the "General Pershing" engines built by the Baldwin Works at their Eddystone Plant during World War I. The model is about 10 feet long.

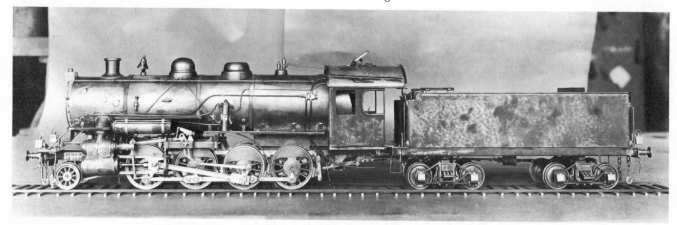

1924

A scale model (12 inches to one foot) of a Reading Pacific. This was built almost entirely of wood, and here is photographed on the boardwalk at Atlantic City for a Miss America Pageant.

1936

This is an Atlantic ¾-inch scale locomotive at a live-steamers' meet at Marblehead, Massachusetts, in 1936. The builder is unknown.

1936

A fine model of a Boston & Albany Hudson, in ¾-inch scale, at the Marblehead meet. The builder is unknown.

1938

A Pennsylvania Railroad K4 Pacific in 1½-inch scale. This was built by Calvert Holt of Greenwich, Connecticut, who also turned out a number of other live-steam engines in various scales.

1939

A 1½-inch-scale model of a Reading Pacific built by apprentices at the company's shops. It was presented by President Edward W. Scheer to the Franklin Institute in Philadelphia.

1940

The Centerville & Southwestern's 2-inch-scale 4-8-4. This is a 9 7/16-inch-gauge locomotive, and is operated over a more than two-mile line at Roseland, New Jersey, in conjunction with the Henry Becker & Son Dairy Farm.

1943

Daniel Boone the 7th built this ¾-inch-scale 4-6-4 in his Blue Ridge Mountain shop.

1950s

Colonel Elliott Springs driving the golden spike inaugurating service on his miniature Lancaster & Chester 15-inch-gauge line. The locomotives were built originally for the Jamestown Exposition in 1904, and appear to be of Cagney make.

162

1950s

Live-steam engines are quite popular in Britain, as these photos indicate. The 4-6-2 "N.E." locomotive is being operated on the Whitefield Model Engineering Society's test track. The young engineman driving the Atlantic engine is at Prestwich annual Sports Day demonstration.

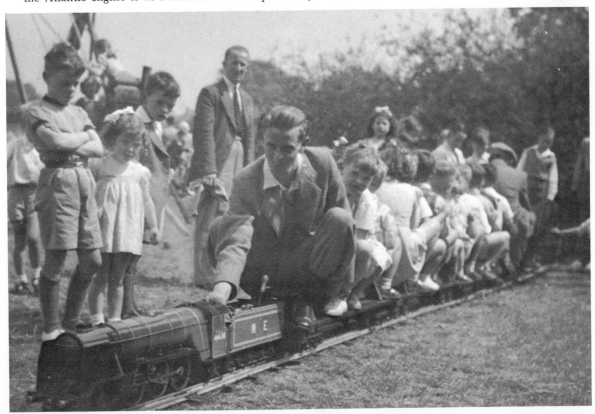

1953

This Atlantic-type engine in ¾-inch scale was built by Frank Godwin, artist and creator of the comic strip "Rusty Riley," at his Solebury, Pennsylvania home.

1959

No. 10 on the author's former Penn Eastern Railroad, built to one eighth actual size, near Yardley, Pennsylvania. This engine was built by William L. Daney in the 1930s and stored for over twenty years, the service on the P.E. being its first. It was slightly altered from its original appearance.

1959

This is the backhead of a much larger engine built by Mr. Frank Godwin—a 1½-inch-scale 4-8-4. This is an oil-fired engine presently owned by Mr. T. C. Marshall of Yorklyn, Delaware.

1960

Mr. T. C. Marshall driving one of the three 4-8-4 engines on his Auburn Valley Railroad, built to one-eighth actual size, at Yorklyn, Delaware.

1960

A 1-inch scale 0-6-0 switcher on the extensive layout of Carl Bellinger on Long Island, New York.

chapter XII

The Locomotive in Many Forms

THE NUMBER OF OBJECTS in the form or carrying the likeness of the iron horse is unbelievable. It indicates how widespread the exploitation of the locomotive theme has been. Collectors of railroadiana have a wide range to specialize in, or they may play the field.

Some of these objects were made in only a few varieties or types; consequently the collecting possibilities are limited. Railroad paperweights are an example—perhaps as many as a hundred different ones have been made, and have been known to collectors since about the time of the Columbian Exposition of 1893, when the Krupp Works souvenir was distributed. In the 1920s a variety of them were made, notably a number of British types. The New York Central had them cast in the forms of the De Witt Clinton and Hudson. A presentation paperweight (not sold but distributed as a gift) was that of the Southern Railway in the form of the "Best Friend of Charleston" of 1831 (page 187). Locomotive companies, too, had such pieces made, the Lima articulated locomotive (page 187) being an excellent example.

Probably the most numerous items in this miscellany are the uniform buttons, most railroads having had at least their own insignia and sometimes locomotives embossed on them. Then there are other types of railroad buttons or badges identifying benefit and other organizations. Along with them may also be grouped the souvenir badges of conventions of railroad associations.

Thousands upon thousands of railroad watches have been made and used, but only a small proportion had either a locomotive pictured on the dial or were engraved on the case. Those that were so decorated make very desirable collectors' items.

Some bookends depicting the iron horse in bas-relief have been made but there are comparatively few. Weathervanes have been mostly custom made; some really rare antiques would be those in the form of old locomotives used on railroad stations or other buildings, but these are difficult to acquire. A recently designed type reproducing the "C. P. Huntington" in deep relief was made available to railroad enthusiasts recently.

Signs in the form of engines are, again, mostly handmade, although some silhouettes of the "General" were produced in cast aluminum. Coupled with the owner's name, such signs indicate without much question the avocation of the resident of a home thus marked. Door knockers, too, in the form of a locomotive would similarly demonstrate an owner's interest, and serve a practical purpose as well.

Charms shaped like old engines were sometimes attached to railroad watches. These were usually individually made, although sometimes a duplicate turns up. Most are old, and some are so complete in detail, despite their smallness, that even wheels and side rods turn. Most of these tiny miniatures were of gold, sometimes encrusted with jewels.

Games showing the iron horse date back to the 1850s, and possibly earlier. Jigsaw puzzles (page 178) were probably the earliest of this type of plaything. Upon the completion of the first transcontinental railroad, a game based upon a cross-country journey was designed. This was lithographed in color, and bore the legend "Col. Geo. Thistleton, Author & Publisher, 1872." Upon a board about two feet square was indicated a track running back and forth between New York and San Francisco. Moving space by space on the board in either direction a theoretical traveler might make the journey along a right of way illustrated with dozens of points of interest (page 182).

Of course, collectors save many items of railroadiana that do not depict the iron horse but that are closely related to it. There are playing cards, switch keys, cigarette cards, models other than those of locomotives; lanterns, books, pamphlets, spikes; locomotive parts such as badge plates, whistles, gauges, bells, and headlights; employee's timetables, brakewheels, signals, postcards, sections of rail; station memorabilia such as clocks, telegraph instruments, and ticket racks; signal-tower items such as diagram boards, levers, indicators, and hoops; and many, many more—even to candy in the form of locomotives.

A railroad enthusiast, bitten hard by the "bug," has an almost limitless variety of objects to seek out and preserve. To him and his quest honoring the iron horse, happy hunting, and may his acquisitions give him all the pleasure so much enjoyed by his fellow collectors.

1830s, 1900

On the right is probably the earliest of all railroad watches. The dial has a hand-painted miniature of a very primitive train in color. The drive, with a minute sprocket chain, is key wound. The maker is Thos. Taylor, Manchester, England. On the left is a railroad watch with a steam locomotive on the dial owned by the vice-president of the Pennsylvania Railroad in charge of electrification of the New York Division.

1830s

A deskset in a fanciful form of a locomotive. The inkwell and thermometer appear obvious; the use of the center container is open to discussion.

Winey Collection

172

1830s

An early miniature representation
of a locomotive that incorporates a
clock.

Winey Collection

173

1830s

Even in the medium of fabrics and needlework the locomotive has not been overlooked. Here are two early examples—a needlepoint design of a 2-2-2 engine and a lace cloth with "Hemfield Rail Road" in the border.

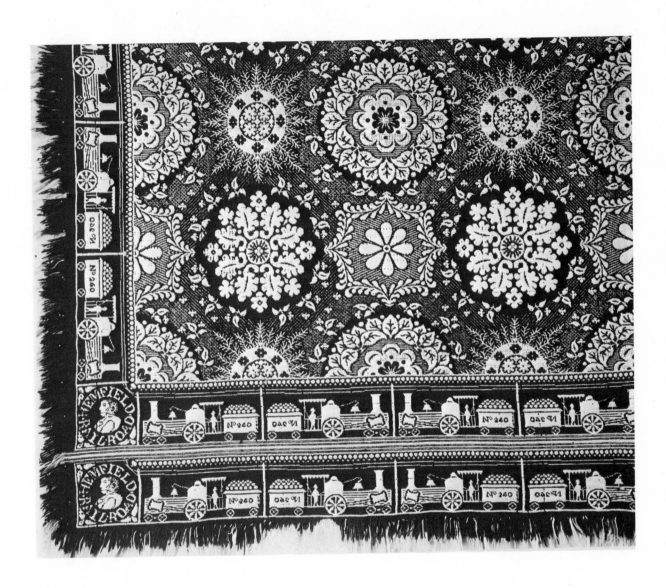

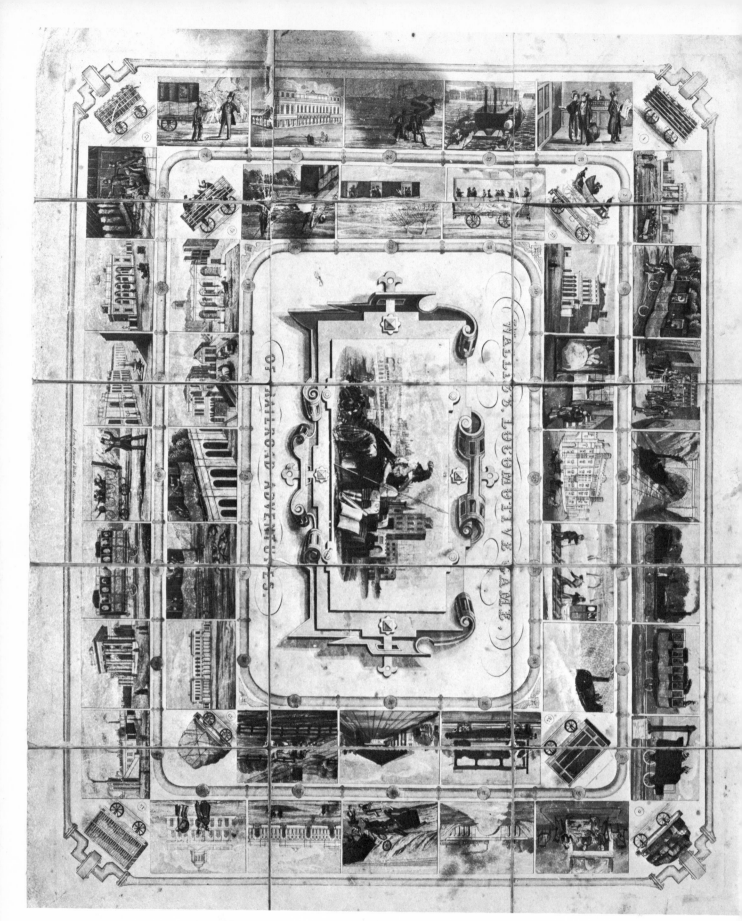

1835

An old railroad game published by Edward Wallis of London.
Ward Kimball Collection

1850s

Silver miniatures of locomotive and cars. These were not toys but objets d'art.
Winey Collection

177

1850s

A jigsaw puzzle with what is supposed to be a Pennsylvania Railroad train. No engine of this system had any locomotive that would even remotely resemble this machine.

Ward Kimball Collection

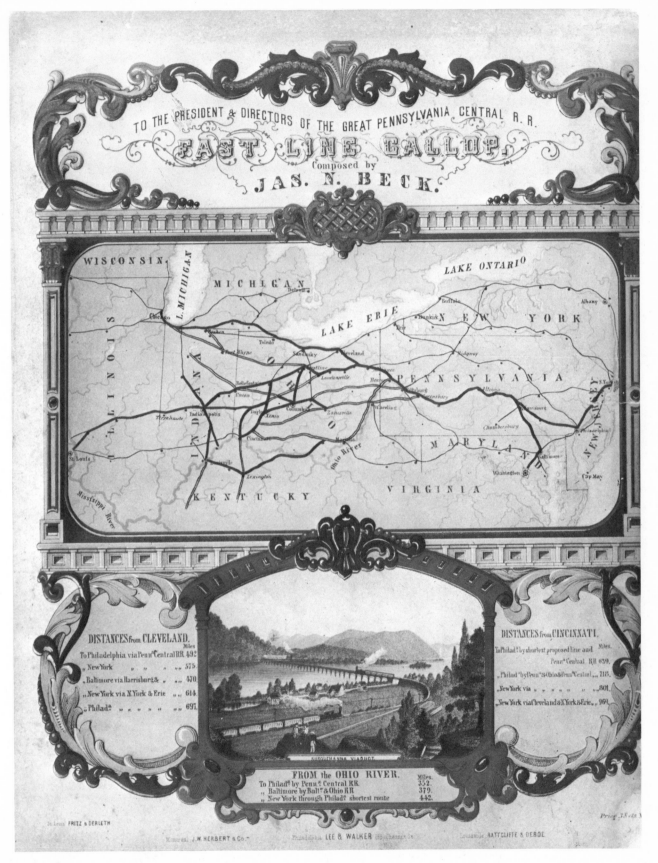

1855

One of the earliest and rarest of sheet-music items relating to railroads is this "Fast Line Gallop" commemorating the new main line of the Pennsylvania Railroad. Note the two trains and the first bridge across the Susquehanna River north of Harrisburg.

1850 to 1890

Thousands of railroad buttons have been made for trainmen, most with the company insignia, but a few with locomotives, as may be seen here.

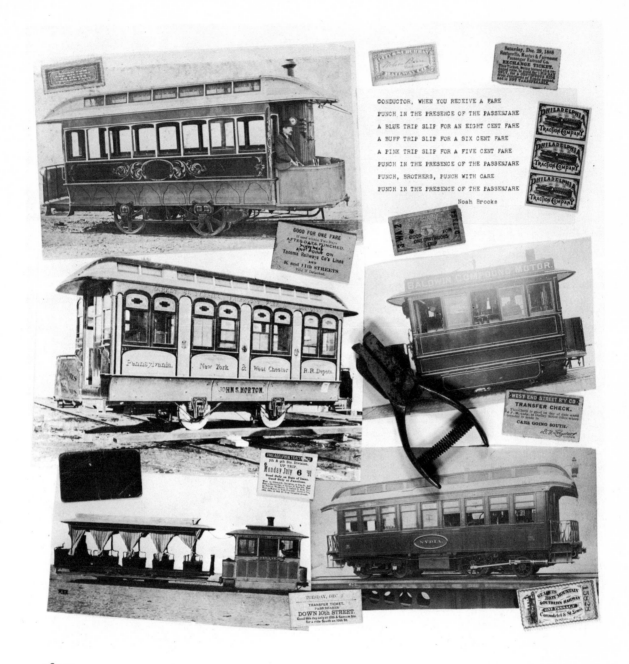

1870s

These are literally the "steam cars"—steam locomotives that are disguised as cars but that also carry passengers. The "dummies," as they were popularly called, were primarily for street railroads, and were designed as cars so that they would not frighten horses as much as actual locomotives did. They were the intermediate link between horse and electric cars between the 1870s and 1890s. Most had vertical boilers and were built by the Baldwin Locomotive Works.

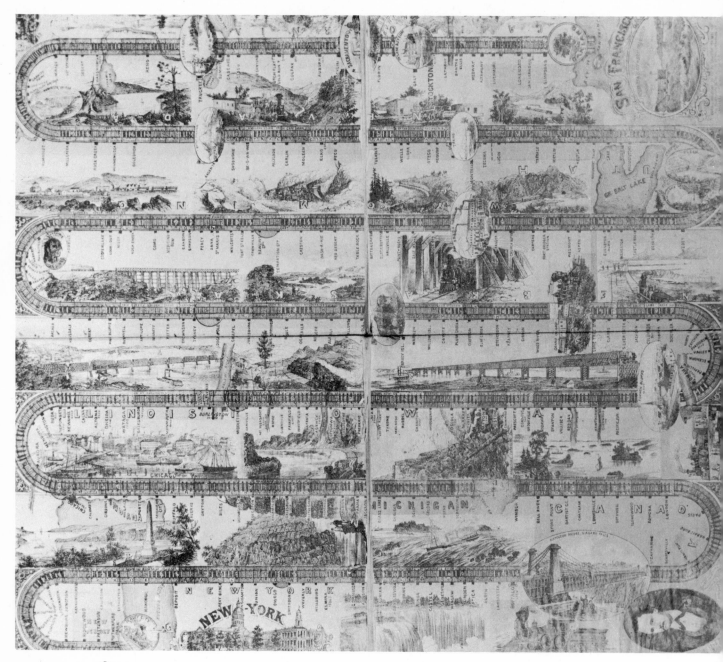

1872

A very unusual railroad game produced shortly after the opening of the first transcontinental railroad. Detailed lithography shows scenes along various railroads from New York to San Francisco.

182

1885

Here are a few railroad watches with locomotives on their cases, and a clock in this form. The engineer and fireman may be seen in the cab.

Ward Kimball Collection

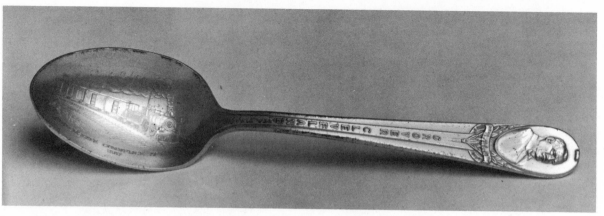

1887

A commemorative spoon showing a train and bearing the likeness of Grover Cleveland.

A. Schrader

1890s

Even tobacco firms used the iron-horse theme in their products. Here is a wrapper from a package of smoking tobacco. Others depicted No. "999"—the Empire State Express—or the De Witt Clinton.

1900s

The locomotive was often part of the theme of the lyrics of popular music. These are covers of sheet music of the 1900s featuring the iron horse in their design.

on Horse entering New Rochelle, N. Y.

Cumberland Valley Depot, Carlisle, Pa.

Electric Train and Steam Locomotive on the N. Y. C. and H. R. R. R.

THE CENTURIES PASSING IN THE NIGHT.

Rockville Bridge, longest Stone Bridge in the World.
Harrisburg, Pa.

Birthday Greetings

MANCHESTER & BLACKPOOL EXPRESS
LANCASHIRE & YORKSHIRE RAILWAY

1900s

Postcards often pictured locomotives. Here are a few from both East and West.

186

1929

Commemorating the chartering of the South Carolina Canal and Railroad Company in 1827, the Southern Railway a hundred years later presented paperweights of the first steam-driven *train* in America, the "Best Friend," in observance. This first ran in 1830, and the South Carolina was the first railroad to publish and operate by a timetable. The "Best Friend" was built in New York by the West Point Foundry. This locomotive paperweight was obtained only by presentation, and not sold.

1920

A variety of paperweights in the form of miniature models of locomotives have been made over many years. On the upper left is a Lima articulated engine, at upper right a British Southern 10-wheeler, at lower left a Reading 4-8-4; at lower right is a Flying Scotsman, and in the lower center a New York Central Hudson.

1927–1945

The steam locomotive will not, of course, be seen on modern timetables, but years ago its likeness frequently appeared on them.

1952

Another reflection of an early iron horse is this door knocker in the form of a Rogers 1860 locomotive. It was finished in polished brass or painted in colors.

Alexander

1930s–1950

An unusual paperweight is this model of a Lionel 402 electric locomotive. At lower left is a matchbox with a miniature train, and at right is a larger one with an illustration of Germany's first locomotive, "Der Adler."

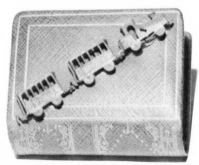

189

Appendixes

*(Railroad Museum and Steam-Passenger
Carriers in the United States)*

*From Compilations of the Association of American Railroads,
Washington, D.C., and* Railroad Magazine, *New York, N.Y.*

It should be noted that these listings are subject to change. New operations are being added and others varying their equipment or schedules. Write ahead of a visit for information, enclosing self-addressed stamped envelope.

ARIZONA

Flagstaff
  Central Arizona Railway. Operates 32 miles southward from Flagstaff. Two steam locomotives.

McNary
  White Mountain Scenic Railroad. About 22 miles. Three steam locomotives.

ARKANSAS

Reader
  Reader Railroad. Three steam locomotives.

CALIFORNIA

Anaheim
  Disneyland & Santa Fe. Four steam locomotives, 3-foot gauge, 1.25 miles. Two other short lines.

Buena Park
  Ghost Town & Calico Railway. Two steam locomotives. 3-foot gauge, 1.5 miles. On Knott's Berry Farm.

Camino
  Camino, Cable & Northern. Five steam locomotives including Shay and Heisler, 3-foot gauge, 1.2 miles.

Felton
  Roaring Camp & Big Trees Narrow Gauge. Two steam locomotives (Shay and Heisler), 3-foot gauge, 3.5 miles.

Los Angeles
  Traveltown in Griffith Park. Outdoor museum with several locomotives, operating narrow gauge.

McCloud
  Mt. Shasta Alpine & Scenic Railway. Fourteen miles, one steam locomotive.

San Gabriel
  Grizzly Flats Railroad. Three steam locomotives, 3-foot gauge, 1,000 feet. The big attraction at Grizzly Flats is the "Emma Nevada," a trimly painted and brilliantly polished Mogul and its equally resplendent coach. On Ward Kimball's San Gabriel estate, where visitors can board the renovated coach that once saw service on the Carson & Colorado

Railroad. The locomotive came from the old Nevada Central Railroad. Write Ward Kimball, 8910 Ardendale Ave. for appointment.

COLORADO

Alamosa, on outskirts of city.
Boasts an intriguing collection of old narrow-gauge equipment and records, including the oldest engine in Colorado. The Narrow Gauge Museum is operated in connection with the Narrow Gauge Motel by Carl A. Heflin and Robert W. Richardson.

Durango
Denver & Rio Grande Western. Three steam locomotives, 3-foot gauge, 45.2 miles. Longest narrow-gauge operation.

Golden
Colorado Railroad Museum. Three-foot gauge, ½ mile. Three steam locomotives, one in operation. Three standard-gauge locomotives on display.

CONNECTICUT

East Windsor
Connecticut Electric Railway. Although primarily a trolley museum with 35 cars, there is some steam operation on over a mile of track. Three steam locomotives.

DELAWARE

Greenbank
Wilmington & Western. Two steam locomotives, 4.5 miles.

DISTRICT OF COLUMBIA

Washington
Smithsonian Institution. Southern Railway's 1401 Pacific and Camden & Amboy John Bull on display in Railroad Hall together with models, etc.

FLORIDA

Hilliard
Nassau County Railway. One steam locomotive, one mile.

Miami
(University of Miami South Campus) Gold Coast Railroad. One steam locomotive, 3.5 miles.

St. Augustine
Florida Southwestern. One steam locomotive (4-6-2), 2-foot gauge, 2 miles.

Silver Springs
Six Gun Territory. Two steam locomotives, 3-foot gauge, 3.5 miles.

GEORGIA

Stone Mountain
Stone Mountain Scenic. Two steam locomotives, 4 miles.

ILLINOIS

Chicago
Chicago Museum of Science and Industry.
Locomotive "Mississippi," owned by Illinois Central, on display.

Union

Illinois Railway Museum. One steam locomotive, ⅔ mile.

INDIANA

Effner

Tee Pee Museum, sponsored by Toledo, Peoria & Western Railroad.

KANSAS

Pittsburg

Schlanger Park, near the Kansas City Southern and Santa Fe rights of way.

KENTUCKY

Louisville

Kentucky Railway Museum, located in Eva Bandman Park.
Sponsored by Louisville chapter of the National Railway Historical Society.

LOUISIANA

Shiloh

Owned by Paulson Spence, president of the Gulf Sand and Gravel Company. Not a public museum, but a 24-hour legal release to tour the property may be obtained. Located two miles south of Amite City on U.S. Highway 51. About 20 steam engines on display.

MAINE

Orono

Historic locomotive "Lion," on display in a transportation museum at the University of Maine—the oldest American-built New England-used locomotive in existence. Built in 1840.

MARYLAND

Baltimore

Baltimore & Ohio Transportation Museum, at Mt. Claire Station. Houses probably the most complete collection of old-time locomotives, many of which are the originals. Also housed in the museum are an extensive collection of railroad insignia and lighting fixtures, and one of the finest existing collections of model railroad bridges.

MASSACHUSETTS

Boston

Railway & Locomotive Historical Society, Baker Library, Harvard Business School, Boston 63, Mass.
Part of the exhibit at this museum has been transferred to the Edaville Railroad Museum, South Carver, Mass. No locomotives on display.

South Carver, near Edaville Station.

Edaville Railroad Museum.
The collection at this 2-foot gauge, 5.5 mile railroad and museum consists of four steam locomotives, gasoline-propelled locomotives, boxcars, flatcars, tank cars, dump cars, cabooses, passenger coaches, observation cars, etc.—and a parlor car believed to be one of the last remaining cars of its kind still in existence.

MICHIGAN

Dearborn
Henry Ford Museum and Greenfield Village.
Contains about eleven locomotives, including one of the largest steam locomotives ever built.

Lake City
Cadillac & Lake City Railroad. Two steam locomotives, 21 miles.

Marquette
Marquette & Huron Mountain Railroad. Eleven steam locomotives, 25 miles.

MINNESOTA

Chisholm
Minnesota Museum of Mining.
On display is DM&I locomotive No. 347, a Consolidation type, built by the Pittsburgh works of the American Locomotive Co.

St. Cloud
Three Great Northern historic cars are on permanent public exhibition.

Two Harbors
One of the early Duluth, Missabe and Iron Range Railway locomotives, familiarly known as the "3 Spot," a woodburner constructed in 1883, is on display at the Paul H. Von Hoven Lake Front Park.

MISSOURI

Independence
Heart of America Railway Museum. One steam locomotive on display.

St. Louis
National Museum of Transport, Inc., Barrette Station Road, St. Louis 22, Missouri.
Has one of the largest collections of old steam locomotives, streetcars, animal-powered cars, electric trains, trolley cars, and buses.

NEBRASKA

Minden
Pioneer Village, built and owned by Harold Warp. The exhibit features such items as early locomotives, oxcarts, prairie schooners, stagecoaches, buggies, bicycles, and streetcars.

Omaha
Union Pacific Museum, located only a few steps off the lobby on the first floor of Union Pacific Railroad's 12-story headquarters building in downtown Omaha. Has an extensive display of documents, maps, and pictures; miniature locomotives, as well as a replica of the Lincoln funeral car. No locomotives.

NEVADA

Carson City
State Museum. Has four engines.

Las Vegas
Last Frontier Village.
On display are several narrow-gauge locomotives.

NEW HAMPSHIRE

Mt. Washington
Mt. Washington Cog Railway. Nine steam locomotives built to climb grades of 37 percent (most in operation), 3.25 miles.

Woodstock
White Mountain Central Railroad. At Clark's Trading Post. Four steam locomotives—Shay, Climax, Heisler, etc., 5 miles.

NEW JERSEY

Allaire State Park
Pine Creek Railroad. Six steam locomotives including an Irish engine, 3-foot gauge, one mile.

Newark
Railroadians of America Museum. Research material but no actual equipment.

Ringoes
Black River & Western. Two steam locomotives, 5 miles of P.R.R. Flemington Branch.

Roseland
Centerville & Southwestern. One steam locomotive (4-8-4), 15-inch gauge, 2 miles.

Whippany
Morris County Central Railroad. Two steam locomotives, 5.5 miles.

NEW YORK

Arcade
Arcade & Attica Railroad. Two steam locomotives, 7 miles.

Cooperstown
Leatherstocking Line. One steam locomotive. Operates on grounds of Woodland Museum.

Livonia
Livonia, Avon & Lakeville. One steam locomotive, 13 miles.

Middletown
Middletown & Orange Railroad. One steam locomotive, 5.5 miles.

Sandy Creek, Oswego County, N.Y.
Rail City Museum, on Lake Ontario, about 35 miles south of Watertown, New York, on the estate of Dr. Stanley A. Groman, a practicing surgeon of Syracuse and an enthusiastic rail fan. Has a steam railroad—both standard- and narrow-gauge track. The museum has about 14 locomotives.

NORTH CAROLINA

Blowing Rock
Tweetsie Railroad. Two steam locomotives, 3-foot gauge, 6 miles.

Fontana Dam
Graham County Railroad. Three steam locomotives (Shay), 3.5 miles (of 12).

Raleigh
Hall of History Railroad in State Department of Archives and History. Display consists of a collection of models that tell the story of railroading in North Carolina.

OHIO

Sandusky
Cedar Point & Lake Erie Railroad. Eight steam locomotives, 3-foot gauge, 1.6 miles.

Worthington
Ohio Railway Museum, designed to preserve relics of Ohio's colorful railroad history. Maintained by rail fans in the Columbus area. Two steam locomotives although primarily a trolley museum, 1.5 miles.

OREGON

Banks
Veronia, South Park & Sunset Railroad. Three steam locomotives, 21 miles.

Portland
Portland Zoo Railroad. One steam locomotive, 30-inch gauge, 1.25 miles.

PENNSYLVANIA

Ashland
Ashland Community Enterprises. One steam locomotive operating into a coal mine, 3-foot gauge.

Blairsville
Penn View Mountain Railroad. A switchback railroad with one steam locomotive.

Bloomsburg
Carroll Park & Western Railroad. Two steam locomotives including a Climax, 4-foot gauge, 2 miles.

Everett
Everett Railroad. Operates 3.5 miles over part of old Huntington & Broad Top Mountain. One steam locomotive.

Kempton
Wanamaker, Kempton & Southern. Two steam locomotives, 3 miles.

New Hope
New Hope & Ivyland Railroad. Three steam locomotives, 16.7 miles.

Northumberland
Pennsylvania Railroad collection, consisting of about 30. items of early railroad rolling stock. Stored—not on exhibition.

Orbisonia
East Broad Top Railroad. Six steam locomotives and two standard-gauge engines, 3-foot gauge, 5 miles.

Philadelphia
Franklin Institute. Two steam locomotives (including Baldwin No. 60,000) on display, railroad exhibits.

Strasburg
Strasburg Railroad. Three steam locomotives, 4.5 miles.

Washington Crossing
Alexander Collection. Models, railroad research material, drawings and photos. Appointment only. Phone 215-493-2231.

York
Rail Tours, Inc. Three steam locomotives, 34 miles of former Maryland & Pennsylvania.

SOUTH DAKOTA

Hill City

Black Hills Central Railroad, operating between Rapid City and Hill City, S.D. A museum dedicated to preserving old steam locomotives. Three steam locomotives, 3-foot and standard gauge.

TENNESSEE

Blowing Rock

Goldrush, Pigeon Forge, Gatlinsburg & Western. One steam locomotive, 3-foot gauge, 5 miles.

Chattanooga

Tennessee Railroad Museum. Steam locomotives and other equipment on display.

Jackson

Casey Jones Museum, owned and operated by the City of Jackson. P.O. Box 382, Jackson, Tenn. The museum contains mementos belonging to Casey Jones, relics and displays of the Casey Jones era, etc. On a track in back of the house is a locomotive similar to the famed engine Old 382, along with tender. The museum is assembled in the same frame house in which Casey Jones lived with his family at the time of the famous train wreck.

TEXAS

Arlington

Six Flags Over Texas. Two or more steam locomotives, 3-foot gauge, one mile.

VERMONT

Bellows Falls

Green Mountain Railroad. Three steam locomotives, 26 miles. At Steamtown Museum, about 40 steam locomotives on display up to U.P. "Big Boy," one of finest collections extant.

Rutland

Vermont Railway. Operates part of former Rutland. One steam locomotive.

Shelburne

Shelburne Museum. On display is Central Vermont locomotive No. 220, "The locomotive of the Presidents."

WASHINGTON

Puget Sound & Snoqualine Valley Railroad. Museum with steam locomotives and other equipment.

WEST VIRGINIA

Cass

Cass Scenic Railroad. Four steam locomotives, all three truck Shays, 4 miles.

WISCONSIN

Green Bay

Wisconsin & Yesterday Railroad. Part of National Railroad Museum. Several steam locomotives, 1 mile.

Laona

Laona & Northern Railway. One steam locomotive.

North Freedom

Rattlesnake & Northern Railroad. Three steam locomotives (one operating).

196

(National in Scope Except as Noted)

OF GENERAL RAILROAD INTEREST
 Locomotive & Railway Historical Society, Boston, Mass.*
 National Railway Historical Society, Lancaster, Pa.*
 Railroad Enthusiasts, New York*
 Railroadians of America, New York*

OLD TOY TRAINS
 Train Collectors' Association, Pittsburgh, Pa.*
 Standard Gauge Association, Somerville, N.J.

OPERATING STEAM LOCOMOTIVES (miniature)
 Brotherhood of Live Steamers, Marblehead, Mass.*
 Southern California Association of Live Steamers

MODEL RAILROADS
 National Model Railroad Association (affiliated clubs in most cities)*

PHOTOGRAPHY
 Engine Picture Club (Railroad Magazine), New York

 * Monthly or quarterly bulletins issued.

(United States and British Ⓑ Monthly except as noted)

LOCOMOTIVE AND RAILROAD   *Founded*
 *Locomotive Engineer *ex* Locomotive Engineering *ex*   1887 (weekly)
  Railway & Locomotive Engineering
 The Locomotive Ⓑ
 *The Railroad & Engineering Journal   1832
 *Railroad Gazette   1856 (weekly)
 Railway Age   (weekly)
 Railway Magazine Ⓑ   1900–
 Railway Mechanical Engineer
 Railroad Magazine *ex* Railroad Stories *ex* Railroad
  Man's Magazine   1907–
 Railway Progress   1946–
 Baldwin Magazine (quarterly)   1922–1943
 Trains   1940–
 *Trains Illustrated   1945
 Modern Railroads

MODELS
 The Model Engineer Ⓑ   1897 to present (weekly)
 *Model Railways & Locomotives Ⓑ   1909
 *The Modelmaker   1924
 Model Railway News Ⓑ   1925 to present
 Railroad Model Craftsman *ex* Model Craftsman   1933 to present
 Model Railroader   1934
 *Mechanical Models   1936
 Railway Modeller   1936
 *Toy Trains   1950
 *The Model Builder (Lionel)
 Model Railway Constructor Ⓑ
 Model Trains *ex* HO Monthly
  *No longer published.

New-Haven Rail Road Co

...ify. that Mathilda J Buck
...ix (26) Shares in the Cap
...ven Rail Road Company of One Ha

State of Connecticut
THE HOUSATONIC RAIL ROAD COM
100,000 DOLLARS OF BONDS SECURED BY MOR

The Housatonic Rail Road Company prom
Levi Eaton
...igns the sum of ONE THOUSAND DOLLARS on the f...
...um hundred and ten and interest from the 1st day of April 188...
...um payable half yearly on the first days of October and April in each year, at the of...
...nt until said principal sum becomes due. This Bond is transferable on the Bo...

Meriden and Cram

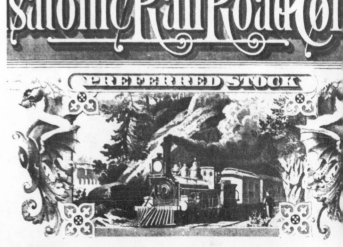

satonic Rail Road Con

PREFERRED STOCK

...John Fletcher